Origin Science

Origin Science

A Proposal for the
Creation-Evolution Controversy

Norman L. Geisler
and J. Kerby Anderson

Foreword by Walter L. Bradley

BAKER BOOK HOUSE
Grand Rapids, Michigan 49506

Copyright 1987 by
Baker Book House Company

ISBN: 0-8010-3808-1

Second printing, July 1987

Library of Congress Catalog Card Number: 86–71864

Printed in the United States of America

Contents

Foreword

Several years ago I had my deposition taken by an ACLU lawyer in preparation for the trial dealing with the Louisiana law requiring balanced treatment of creation and evolution in public schools. Two of his questions well illustrate the type of confusion of categories that fuels the current creation-evolution controversy. First, he asked me how I could be an objective scientist and maintain a Christian world view with a belief in the supernatural. Implicit in his question is the idea that science deals only with so-called natural processes and is necessarily blind to the supernatural (if indeed such exists at all). Didn't that put me in a compromising position? I answered the question by indicating that in fact my Christian world view makes me more open-minded and objective than the scientist with an atheistic world view. If the goal of science is to seek cause-and-effect relationships in the multitude of phenomena we observe, then to assume a priori that all effects must have natural causes is prejudicial and will be counterproductive, if indeed some phenomena (present or past) are the result of a supernatural cause.

The attorney's second question indicated that my belief that a supernatural cause is required to explain the origin of life cannot be scientific, since it is not falsifiable. I responded that one may easily falsify my hypothesis of a supernatural origin of life by running a successful prebiotic simulation experiment in which a simple living system is assembled, under conditions which meaningfully simulate the early earth's biosphere, without undue investigator interference. Although such an experiment would not prove this was the actual biochemical path taken originally, it would demonstrate that natural processes can produce the required complexity for a simple living system. However, falsifying a belief in a naturalistic origin of life is far more difficult, I explained, because an unsuccessful experiment proves only that a given pathway would not work. But an infinite number of pathways could be proposed. Thus, one needs to argue not on the basis of unsuccessful experiments alone but on the basis of fundamental principles that naturalistic explanations are inadequate at present.

Such a position is necessarily tentative in that a new, natural, information-generating principle in nature might be discovered in the future. But this is true of all scientific laws, theories, and hypotheses. New understanding could render any current scientific theory false.

In light of the ideas developed in this book, today I would add that all one needs to do to falsify a creationist view of origins is to show that there are no significant similarities between specified complexity, such as is regularly produced by intelligent causes in the present, and that which was plausibly present in the first living organism. Or, show that specified complexity does not regularly flow from an intelligent cause in the present. For if the first living organism had specified complexity, similar to that found to regularly result from an intelligent cause in the present, then, as Geisler and Anderson argue, it is plausible to postulate an intelligent creator of life.

The lawyer's questions were undoubtedly generated from discussions with scientific experts hired by the ACLU and reflect the belief of many scientists that science and the supernatural are mutually exclusive categories of human thought and understanding, with the supernatural being relegated to the sphere of speculative philosophy or religion. If this be so, then the ACLU is right in its contention that teaching creationism in the classroom is tantamount to bootlegging religion into science classes. But are science and the supernatural always mutually exclusive? Must we assume all effects have only natural causes?

Geisler and Anderson in *Origin Science* provide a penetrating analysis of this question. Using a combination of history of science and philosophy of science, they trace the gradual shift in thinking during the past three centuries that has brought us to the widely held belief that science is the realm of naturalism alone. More importantly, they provide for the reader an insightful critique of this position, exposing its inherent inconsistencies and its inability to "deal with the data" when one considers the origin of the universe, life, and complex life forms.

Helpful discussions of theism versus naturalism are provided, along with a careful analysis of the various positions taken by theists (including theistic evolutionism, progressive creationism, and mature creationism). The distinction between primary and secondary causes is explored. The appendices contain a stimulating update of William Paley's classical theistic argument from design and the minority opinion of the seven appeals-court judges who supported the law requiring the balanced treatment of creation and evolution in Louisiana.

For the person interested in understanding the fundamental issues at stake in the creation-evolution controversy (as opposed to the technical details), I highly recommend this book.

Walter L. *Bradley*
Texas A & M University

Acknowledgments

W e are grateful for the assistance given us by many scholars, including Richard Aulie, Walter Bradley, Duane Gish, and Dean Kenyon, in the preparation of this manuscript.

We are also grateful for the valuable help provided by Charles Thaxton, especially on the last two chapters. The terms *forensic science* and *origin science* were used in the excellent book by Thaxton, Bradley, and Olsen, *The Mystery of Life's Origin* (1984).* Many of the ideas expressed in this volume were conceived as the result of numerous hours of fruitful dialogue with Thaxton on the question of origins. We, of course, are responsible for the thoughts expressed in the following pages.

---

*Similar terms, such as "science of origins," can be found in Norman L. Geisler, Is *Man the Measure?* (1983).

Introduction

Like ships passing in the night, creationists and evolutionists continue on their own separate courses, each believing the other is headed in the wrong direction. Evolutionists claim creationist views are not science but religion. Creationists respond in kind, calling evolution a myth or a religion. Evolutionists claim creation is not science because it interjects the supernatural into natural science. Creationists respond by claiming evolution is incurably and unjustifiably naturalistic. On and on the battle goes, with little common ground and, on the popular level, almost no understanding of what the opposing party believes.

It is the thesis of this book that the misunderstanding arises in part because of the confusion of different kinds of science. Science as normally understood deals with regularities, that is, with regularly recurring patterns of events against which theories can be tested. Thus a theory can be falsified or proven wrong if it does not measure up against the regularly recurring patterns in nature. Usually these regular patterns are observable in the present (e.g., the law of gravity). At other times these patterns occurred in the past and must be assumed by way of the principle of uniformity (which says "the present is the key to the past"). Direct observation of the regular pattern is not necessary so long as there is such a pattern and so long as the theory can in some way be measured against it.

But not all science deals with regular recurring patterns in the present or past. Some events of significance to scientists are singularities. These are unique events which so far as can be ascertained happened only once, or at least are not recurring. Some of these events occur (or may occur) in the present. The search for extra-terrestrial intelligence (SETI) by means of powerful radio telescopes is an example. As the well-known astronomer Carl Sagan put it, the discovery of "a *single* message" from outer space would verify the existence of some super intelligence (1979, 275, emphasis added).

Now the science which deals with singularities, such as a single coded message from space, is obviously different from one which deals with a recurring pattern of events. In fact, such an event as a message from space demands positing a primary (intelligent) cause as opposed to a secondary (natural) cause which is laid down for a regularly recurring pattern of events in nature. A similar situation arises when a geologist is confronted with a singularity on a moun-tainside, such as the faces on Mount Rushmore. Since this phe-nomenon is not recurring, the scientist must have a way of positing a cause for it without being able to observe a recurring series of Mount Rushmores. This is true whether the singularity happens in the pres-ent (such as a message from an extraterrestrial) or whether it oc-curred in the past (such as Mount Rushmore). If it occurs in the present, then observation is a key factor. If it happened in the unob-served past, then the scientific approach to it will be more like a forensic science than an empirical science. That is, the scientist will have to reconstruct the unobserved past singularity on the basis of knowledge he has from the present.

It is the proposal of this book that a science which deals with origin events does not fall within the category of empirical science, which deals with observed regularities in the present. Rather, it is more like a forensic science, which concentrates on unobserved sin-gularities in the past. That is, a science about origins is a singularity science about the past; it differs from a scientific understanding about singularities in the present (see appendix 3). A science about the past does not observe the past singularity but must depend on the principle of uniformity (analogy), as historical geology and ar-chaeology do. That is, since these kinds of sciences deal with unob-served past events (whether regular or singular), those events can be "known" only in terms of like events in the present. Thus when a geologist sees a deposit in the rocks whch resembles one observed to result from flooding, erosion, or sedimentation in the present, he can plausibly posit a similar secondary (natural) cause for the unob-served past event. Likewise, when an archaeologist discovers a single coin or work of art in ancient strata he can by analogy with the present legitimately assume that it had a primary (intelligent) cause.

The great events of origin were singularities. The origin of the universe is not recurring. Nor is the origin of life, or the origin of major new forms of life. These are past singularities over which creationists and evolutionists debate. Evolutionists posit a secondary natural cause for them; creationists argue for a supernatural primary cause. The proposal of this book is that both "evolutionist" and "creationist" views (see appendix 2) on origin should be brought into the domain of singularity science about the past and that each should be judged by the principles of that kind of science. Such a science about past singularities will be called "science of origin" (Geisler 1983a, 135), or "origin science" (Thaxton, Bradley, and Olsen 1984, 204). It will be differentiated from science about present regularities (called operation science) in that the latter focuses on a recurring pattern of events in the present against which its theories can be tested; the former does not.

There are really four basic categories (see fig. 1). Two of these approaches deal with regularities and two with singularities. But since the focus in the creation-evolution debate is on past origins, it will be most useful to concentrate on the contrast between origin science and operation science.

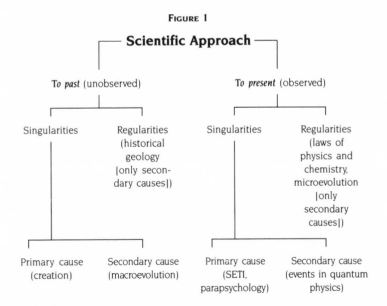

FIGURE 1

Scientific Approach

To *past* (unobserved)

Singularities

Regularities (historical geology [only secondary causes])

Primary cause (creation)

Secondary cause (macroevolution)

To *present* (observed)

Singularities

Regularities (laws of physics and chemistry, microevolution [only secondary causes])

Primary cause (SETI, parapsychology)

Secondary cause (events in quantum physics)

In origin science it is necessary to find analogies in the present to these events of the past (see chap. 6). Thus, for example, if evidence is forthcoming that life can now be synthesized from chemicals (without intelligent manipulation) under conditions similar to those reasonably assumed to have once existed on the primitive earth, then a naturalistic (secondary-cause) explanation of the origin of life is plausible. If, on the other hand, it can be shown that the kind of complex information found in a living cell is similar to that which can be regularly produced by an intelligent (primary) cause, then it can be plausibly argued that there was an intelligent cause of the first living organism (see chap. 7). The situation may be diagrammed as in figure 2.*

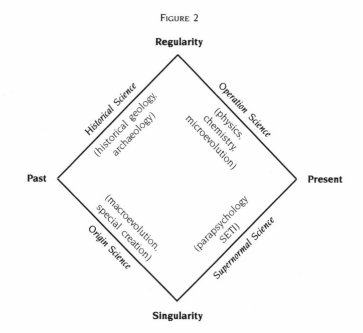

FIGURE 2

From this it can be seen that science can deal with both the present and the past, with both regularities and singularities. However, when the object of study is a regularity it always has a secondary (natural) cause. Only when the object of scientific analysis is a sin-

*See also Thaxton 1985.

gularity is it possible to have a direct primary cause. For when there is a regular pattern of events against which to test a theory, then there will always be a natural cause. Citing God's special intervention to explain regularly recurring events is to argue for a deus ex machina; it is an illegitimate God-of-the-gaps move. On the other hand, assuming all singularities have natural causes is an unwarranted bias against the supernatural. Natural causes can be legitimately posited only where there is a known constant conjunction between that kind of event and a natural cause. When, on the other hand, it is known that there is a constant conjunction between a primary intelligent cause and a certain kind of event, then it is plausible to posit such a cause for a similar kind of past singularity.

The belief in a supernatural primary cause of the universe and living things was part of the scientific world for its earliest two-and-a-half centuries (see chap. 1). However, with the rise of success in the domain of empirical science, the belief in supernatural intervention diminished to near zero among scientists (see chaps. 2–4). The reason for this naturalistic bent is that science came to be identified with the study of regularities (empirical science) which admits of only secondary (natural) causes (chap. 5). However, with the formulation of the big bang theory, attention has again been focused on singularities. This means that some scientists are willing to again accept the plausibility of a primary-cause (creationist) view of origins (chap. 6). Such a view, following the guidelines of operation science about the past, is outlined in chapter 7.

Our proposal, then, is that there are two basic kinds of scientific explanations: primary causes and secondary causes. Likewise, there are two basic kinds of events: regularities and singularities, either of which may occur in the past or the present. It is clear that natural (secondary) causes are the only legitimate kinds of causes to posit for a regular recurring pattern of events. However, singularities, whether past or present (see appendix 3), can have a primary or supernatural cause. But whether they have a supernatural or a natural cause, past singularities come within the province of origin science.

It is our hope that this proposal for treating the study of origins under the special category of origin science—whether by evolutionists or creationists—will reopen meaningful dialogue on this age-old debate. At least the "ships" of evolution and creation need not pass in the night; adherents of each view can discuss the issue of origins in the light of this distinction between origin science and operation science.

In view of this it seems evident that the creation-evolution discussion will be fruitless unless the present equivocal use of the term *science* is rejected. For example, it is misleading to call macroevolution science in the same sense that microevolution is science. Microevolution is a recurring pattern in the present, whereas macroevolution involves singularities of the past. Likewise, it is unfair to claim, as evolutionists sometimes do, that creation is not science in the same sense that macroevolution is science, for both deal with unrepeated singularities of the past. Neither can be tested against the origin events. Neither has as its object some recurring pattern of events in the present. In brief, neither is an object of operation science. Rather, both are the subject of origin science (see chap. 6). Unless there can be agreement on this issue, there will probably be no real meeting of minds in the continued dialogue between creation and evolution.

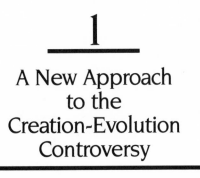

1

A New Approach to the Creation-Evolution Controversy

The Current Controversy

The Resurgence of Creationist Views

Creationist views among scholars declined sharply after Charles Darwin's views became well known. During the Darwin centennial celebration in Chicago (Nov. 26, 1959) Julian Huxley declared, "In the evolutionary pattern of thought there is no longer need or room for the supernatural. The earth was not created; it evolved. So did all the animals and plants that inhabit it, including our human selves, mind and soul as well as brain and body. So did religion." Overzealous utterances such as these would probably have been muted had their speaker known what reaction was about to be unleashed upon the English-speaking world.

The beginning of the modern creationist resurgence is usually traced to 1961, when *The Genesis Flood*, by Henry M. Morris and John C. Whitcomb, was published. By 1980 more than one hundred thousand copies had been distributed. For more than a decade the scientific establishment ignored this band of "scientific fundamentalists," hoping it would self-destruct or just go away. It did neither. Unlike their forebears in the 1920s, many creationists have been scientifically trained at some of the most respected universities.

After publication of Morris's and Whitcomb's book and the founding of the *Creation Research Society Quarterly* (1964–present), there followed a raft of creationist books. Some of the more well-known works include *Scientific Creationism* (1974), edited by Henry M. Morris; *Evolu-*

tion? The Fossils Say No! (1973) by Duane T. Gish; Man's Origin, Man's
Destiny (1968) by A. E. Wilder-Smith; The Creation-Evolution Controversy
(1976) by R. L. Wysong; Fossils in Focus (1977) by J. Kerby Anderson and
Harold Coffin; The Neck of the Giraffe (1982) by Francis Hitching; A Case
for Creation (1983) by Wayne Friar and Percival Davis; Scientific Studies in
Special Creation (1971), edited by Walter Lammerts; and Biology (1970),
edited by John N. Moore and Harold Slusher.

Numerous creationist organizations arose during this same pe-
riod; these include the Creation Research Society (Ann Arbor), the
Institute for Creation Research (El Cajon, Calif.), Students for Origin
Research (Santa Barbara, Calif.), and the Bible-Science Association
(Minneapolis).

In the 1970s creationists participated in debates with prominent
evolutionists on many university campuses, and a few became politi-
cally active in sponsoring legislation in numerous states that would
require public schools to teach creation along with evolution in science classes, if either view is taught. The state of Arkansas passed
such a bill (Act 590) which was signed into law on March 19, 1981. In
this law "creation-science" was defined as

> the scientific evidences for creation and inferences from those scien-
> tific evidences. Creation-science includes the scientific evidences and
> related inferences that indicate: (1) Sudden creation of the universe,
> energy, and life from nothing; (2) The insufficiency of mutation and
> natural selection in bringing about development of all living kinds
> from a single organism; (3) Changes only within fixed limits of orig-
> inally created kinds of plants and animals; (4) Separate ancestry for man
> and apes; (5) Explanation of the earth's geology by catastrophism, includ-
> ing the occurrence of a worldwide flood; and (6) A relatively recent incep-
> tion of the earth and living kinds. (Cited in Geisler 1982a, 5.)

A similar law that was passed in Louisiana (Senate Bill No. 86,
1981) defined creation science more simply, saying, "'Creation-
science' means the scientific evidences for creation and inferences
from those scientific evidences" (ibid., 224).

The Reaction to Creation Science

The legal establishment has reacted strongly to the rise of creationist views. Federal courts ruled against the teaching of creation

science in both Arkansas and Louisiana. The Arkansas decision came on January 5, 1982. It holds, in part, that the essential characteristics of science are that

1. It is guided by natural law;
2. It has to be explanatory by reference to natural law;
3. It is testable against the empirical world;
4. Its conclusions are tentative, i.e., are not necessarily the final word; and
5. It is falsifiable.

Having thus defined science the judge declared,

> Creation science as described in Section 4(a) fails to meet these essential characteristics. First, the section revolves around 4(a)(1) which asserts a sudden creation "from nothing." Such a concept is not science because it depends upon a supernatural intervention which is not guided by natural law. It not explanatory by reference to natural law, is not testable and is not falsifiable. (Ibid., 176)*

The judge in the Louisiana case declined to decide on whether creationist views are scientific but ruled that

> whatever "science" may be, "creation," as the term is used in the statute, involves religion, and the teaching of "creation-science" and "creationism," as contemplated by the statute, involves teaching "tailored to the principles" of a particular religious sect or group of sects (Epperson . . . 1968). As it is ordinarily understood, the term "creation" means the bringing into existence of mankind and of the universe and implies a divine creator. While all religions may not teach the existence of a supreme being, a belief in a supreme being (a creator) is generally considered to be a religious tenet (Don Aguillard, Jan. 10, 1985).†

The reaction of the academic and scientific establishments also has been emphatic. Many groups have denounced the teaching of creation science. The American Association of University Professors

---

*An eyewitness, documented account of this trial is found in Norman L. Geisler, *The Creator in the Courtroom* (1982).

†This case was appealed and lost by only one vote on a split decision. See appendix 4.

devoted an issue of *Academe* to consideration of "creationism and the classroom." The AAUP passed a resolution which reads,

> This legislation, by requiring that a religious doctrine (sometimes disguised) be taught as a condition for the teaching of science, serves to impair the soundness of scientific education preparatory for college study and to violate the academic freedom of public school teachers. . . . The Sixty-seventh Annual Meeting of the American Association of University Professors calls on state governments to reject "creation-science" legislation as utterly inconsistent with the principles of academic freedom. (*Academe*, March-April 1982, 7)

The council of the National Academy of Sciences in 1981 passed a resolution which stated, "Religion and science are separate and mutually exclusive realms of human thought whose presentation in the same context leads to misunderstanding of both scientific theory and religious belief." (This resolution was reaffirmed in *Science and Creationism* [1984], a publication of the NAS.) The "unequivocal conclusion" of the NAS is "that creationism, with its account of the origin of life by supernatural means, is not science . . . that the tenets of 'creation science' are not supported by scientific evidence, that creationism has no place in a *science* curriculum at any level" (pp. 6, 26).

A joint resolution of the board and council of the American Association for the Advancement of Science stated that "because 'creationist science' has no scientific validity it should not be taught as science. . ." (*Science* 215, 1072).

The board of directors of the American Chemical Society in 1981 reaffirmed its 1972 statement "that creationism theories, often mistermed 'scientific creationism,' should not be taught as science in the nation's science classes."*

In August 1986, seventy-two evolutionists, all Nobel Prize-winners, urged the Supreme Court to declare the teaching of creation science unconstitutional in public schools.

The scientific community has also responded to the advances of creation science with a host of books by evolutionists, including *Abusing Science* (1982) by Philip Kitcher; *Science on Trial* (1982) by Douglas J. Futuyma; *The Monkey Business* (1982) by Niles Eldredge; *Is God a*

---

*From the December 6, 1981, minutes of the board of directors of the American Chemical Society, 1155 Sixteenth Street, N.W., Washington, D.C. 20036.

Creationist? (1983), edited by Roland M. Frye; *Scientists Confront Creationism* (1983), edited by Laurie R. Godfrey; *Creation and Evolution* (1982) by Norman D. Newell; *Did the Devil Make Darwin Do It?* (1983), edited by David B. Wilson; *Creationism, Science, and the Law* (1983), edited by Marcel la Follette; *Science and Creationism* (1984), edited by Ashley Montagu; and *Creationism on Trial* (1985) by Langdon Gilkey, among others.

These books make the same two basic points as do the court decisions: creation is not really science, and creation is a religious belief. As to the first point the comments of Philip Kitcher are noteworthy. He agrees with the conclusion of Theodosius Dobzhansky that "nothing in biology makes sense except in the light of evolution" (Kitcher 1982, 54). Further, he adds,

> creation "science" is spurious science. To treat it as science we would have to overlook its intolerable vagueness. We would have to abandon large parts of well-established sciences (physics, chemistry, and geology, as well as evolutionary biology, are all candidates for revision). . . . There is not a single scientific question to which Creationism provides its own detailed problem solution. In short, Creationism could take a place among the sciences only if the substance and methods of contemporary science were mutilated to make room for a scientifically worthless doctrine.

In contrast, says Kitcher, evolutionary theories are good science because they "constantly make claims that are subject to independent check" (ibid., 52). In short, "a straightforward evolutionary story makes sense of what we observe" (ibid., 57). So these critics of creation science maintain that evolution is valid science because its theories are subject to testing against the natural world, whereas creationist views are not. Instead of giving a scientific explanation, creationists affirm the work of a primary supernatural Creator, which critics maintain is an object of religion, not of science.

A Response to Criticisms of Creationist Views

The two basic criticisms of creationist views are that they are not truly science, and that they are religious and therefore should be excluded from the science curriculum. These criticisms will be considered in order. We will draw freely on the distinction between operation science and origin science that was made in the introduction and that will be elaborated in the following chapters.

Are Creationist Views Unscientific?

Several objections are given to teaching creationist views as science.

First, if primary-cause creation is taught, say the critics, then how can we avoid teaching the flat-earth theory in geography and the Greek four-element theory in chemistry?

This commonly raised objection is answered by first noting that the phenomena in question, that is, the shape of the earth and the behavior of matter, deal with regularities. They are open to regular observation. Therefore they qualify as objects of study in operation science, which deals with only natural (secondary) causes. Theories about recurrent patterns of events are falsifiable, and these particular theories of a flat earth and four-element matter have been empirically tested and falsified. These are the proper domain of operation science (see introduction and chap. 6). We should not teach as operation science testable but falsified theories. Hence, flat-earth and four-element theories should not be taught as science.

Astrology and the demon theory of disease are sometimes included in lists of additional viewpoints that must be included in school curricula if origin science is permitted a place. But these too should be excluded entirely from either operation science or origin science. Neither astrology nor medicine (disease) deals with the origins of the universe of living things. Also, positing demonic causes is not part of operation science. The demon theory of diseases can no more be empirically tested than the belief that one's watch is caused to operate by an invisible green gremlin.*

Second, critics charge that teaching about special creation is not based on any presently observed regularities in nature and hence is not science.

It is true that special creation is not testable against any regularly recurring pattern of events in the present. But neither is macroevolution. Both views involve unobserved past singularities (see chap. 6).

---

*See appendix 3 for a discussion of supernormal singularities as opposed to normal or regular patterns involved in disease theory.

That is, they involve rare occurrences. For example, so far as we can tell, life did not emerge from nonlife over and over. Nor were the great transitions between major forms of life repeated again and again. Hence there are no recurring patterns of events against which to test how the universe began, how life began, or how diverse life forms originated. So neither macroevolution nor creation comes within the discipline of operation science. This does not mean there is no sense in which macroevolution and creation are scientific. Although they are not an empirical science, nevertheless they function like a forensic science. Just as a forensic scientist tries to make a plausible reconstruction of an unobserved (and unrepeatable) murder, so the evolutionist and creationist attempt to construct a plausible scenario of the unobserved past singularities of origin. So neither view is operation science. Rather, both are in the domain of origin science (see introduction).

Third, critics object that special creation is not verifiable or falsifiable and therefore is unscientific.

In the strict scientific sense, it is true that special creation is not falsifiable. But neither is macroevolution. For neither theory involves a recurring pattern of events in the present against which empirical tests can be made.* Both macroevolution and creation deal with unobserved past singularities. Origin theories are thus evaluated differently than operational theories are.

However, there is an indirect way to "test" these past events, not in any strict empirical sense, but in the same way a forensic scientist can "test" scenarios. The forensic scientist uses certain principles, such as causality and uniformity (analogy), and relies too on the persuasive power of circumstantial evidence in presenting a case (see chaps. 6–7). He assumes every event has an adequate cause. Further, causes observed to be constantly conjoined to certain kinds of events in the present are probably the same kind of causes that similar past events had. Thus, if evolutionists can find a natural cause (such as natural selection) in the present which can repeatedly produce certain kinds of changes in living organisms, then they may legitimately assume that similar kinds of changes resulted from a similiar cause in the past. In this indirect way a theory of macroevolution can be "tested."

---

*Microevolution is an empirical science, since it can be observed in the present (see chap 7).

However, it cannot be tested in any direct empirical way, because origin events are not recurring in the present and hence are not available to measure a theory of macroevolution against.

Neither can special creation be tested in any direct empirical way, because it too deals with past singularities and not recurring patterns which can be observed in the present. But like macroevolution, special creation can be "tested" in an indirect forensic way by applying the principles of causality and uniformity (analogy) and amassing circumstantial evidence in a persuasive manner. If it can be shown that a primary intelligent cause is capable of regularly producing the kind of complex information found in a living cell, then it can be assumed that a similar kind of intelligent cause could have produced that kind of effect in the past (see chap. 7). So here too the plausible reconstruction of an unobserved past singularity may be posited in accordance with present, observed constant conjunctions of certain kinds of causes and certain kinds of effects. In this indirect way both macroevolution and creation theories can be "tested" to see whether they are plausible or implausible. And plausibility is judged by the closeness of the analogy. But neither macroevolution nor primary-cause creation can be tested or falsified in the strict empirical sense of the words.

Fourth, critics insist that science deals only with natural phenomena and causes, not a supernatural primary cause.

It is true that empirical or operation science deals only with natural secondary causes because only here are there recurring patterns of events by which scientific theories can be tested. Primary intelligent causes are not bound by law, but transcend law. Hence it is perfectly legitimate to explain the operation of the universe in terms of purely natural secondary causes. However, science has no right as science to place the same limits on explanations of the origin of the universe and of living things. Ultimate origins are beyond the scope of empirical, operation science for two reasons. First, the origin events are not available for observation by scientists. Second, they form no recurring pattern of events by which scientists can test theories. Therefore origins are outside the domain of operation science. To posit only natural secondary causes for origins mistakenly treats origins as if they were part of the sphere of operation science.

A good case in point is the big bang hypothesis, which holds that the universe came into existence at a definite moment in the finite past. Empirical, operation-science methods may be used in origin science, and can be used (by way of observing an expanding universe, a radiation echo, and the running down of the universe) to show there was a first event of the natural world, but beyond that these methods cannot go. As Robert Jastrow put it,

> Astronomers now find they have painted themselves into a corner because they have proven, by their own methods, that the world began abruptly in an act of creation to which you can trace the seeds of every star, every planet, every living thing in this cosmos and on the earth. And they have found that all this happened as a product of forces they cannot hope to discover. (1982, 15)

But Jastrow here writes as if he is dealing with operation science. Actually he is discussing origin events but using operation-science methods. He thus arrives at a conundrum, that is, how to use operation-science methods to say something meaningful about origins.

Allan Sandage expresses the same dilemma when he says, "Astronomers may have found the first effect, but not, thereby, necessarily the first cause sought by Anselm and Aquinas" (1985, 54). The reason for this is simply that "knowledge of the creation is *not* knowledge of the Creator. . . ." That is to say, operation science by its very nature is limited. It can provide insights into the operation of the universe by secondary natural causes, but cannot offer insights about the origin of the universe. However, origin science, which, like a forensic science, deals with unobserved past singularities rather than present regularities, may consider both natural and supernatural causes.

Fifth, some have argued that "the question of secondary causes . . . is the *scientific* question; the question of primary cause is the *religious* question—and they are quite different questions" (Gilkey 1982, 50). Hence they insist one is wrong when "all are regarded as theories of the *same* sorts of truth" (ibid., 35).

There are several serious difficulties with this argument:

1. It assumes without justification that all events within the universe can be explained in terms of secondary (natural) causes. But this is a metaphysical (philosophical) assumption, not a purely scientific one.
2. It is an arbitrary definition of science. Who said that science should only posit secondary causes for origins? What if there are no plausible grounds for positing anything but a primary

cause for an event (such as an intelligent architect for the pyramids)?

3. It is based on a failure to recognize the difference between operation science (which deals only with secondary causes) and origin science (which does not).

4. It was a common practice among early modern scientists (before the twentieth century) to posit a primary cause for origin events. Hence, contrary to the critics, the scientific propriety of a creationist view of origins is rooted in the history of science.

This objection says that to posit a Creator is to stop looking for a scientific explanation. This negates the motivation to do research. In response, it should be noted that this would be true only if the interventions of a creator are used to explain phenomena in operation science, as Isaac Newton did to explain the perturbed orbits of some planets. This is a God-of-the-gaps move which has no place in explaining the operation of the universe. For all operational laws are based on a recurring pattern of events against which operation-science theories can be tested. Invoking primary-cause interventions to explain recurring patterns of events is a violation of operation science. It is to invoke a deus ex machina. Just because scientists did not know the natural causes of meteors, eclipses, volcanic eruptions, and the bumblebee's flight did not justify positing the direct intervention of God to explain these recurring natural events. Indeed, subsequent natural explanations have been found for all these phenomena. The operation scientist is justified in believing that natural explanations will yet be found for some present anomalies in the operation of nature (such as how life is sustained in the dark high-pressure depths around sea-floor hydrothermal vents).

However, just because it is improper to invoke the interventions of a Creator to explain the anomalies of the operation of the world does not mean it is also wrong to posit a creator for the origin of the world and life. Origin science does not deal with observed present regularities but with unobserved past singularities. Hence, positing a primary cause of origins is not a violation of operation science, any more than claiming an intelligent cause of the origin of a motor is a violation of the laws by which a motor operates. Just as the natural laws by which a motor functions do not account for the genesis of a motor, so too the natural laws by which the universe operates need not be the means by which it originated. So positing a Creator of the beginning of the universe and life in no way violates the study of the natural laws of the running of the universe.

Seventh, critics object that the argument from design is cogent but is not science.

Many scientists grant the cogency of the argument from design. For example, Sandage confessed his acceptance of the force of the argument, declaring,

> . . . the world is too complicated in all its parts and interconnections to be due to chance alone. I am convinced that the existence of life with all its order in each of its organisms is simply too well put together. Each part of a living thing depends on all its other parts to function. How does each part know? How is each part specified at conception? The more one learns of biochemistry the more unbelievable it becomes unless there is some type of organizing principle—an architect. (1985, 54)

But not all scientists who argue this way imply that such an argument is part of science. It may be cogent but it is not science; it transcends science.

In response it should be acknowledged that the objection has validity if one is speaking of operation science. For operation science as such deals with how the universe functions, not why. Teleology is not formally a part of empirical science. Such scientific pursuits are not concerned with ends but with means. They are concerned with the process, not with any alleged product (goal) of it. However, although operation science as such is not concerned about why something was designed, origin science is interested in who (or what) produced it.

Perhaps it is a confusion of teleology (end) and causality (cause) which distracts the modern scientific mind from seeing this point. Origin science as such is not interested in why (purpose) the universe or life was produced but who or what (cause) brought it to be. Origin science deals with the efficient cause, not the final cause of things.* To be sure, if some intelligence created life, then there was no doubt a

---

*This distinction is overlooked by Robert B. Fisher in *God Did It, But How?* (1981) and this invalidates his main thesis.

purpose for so doing. But purpose (why) is no more a formal part of origin science (which asks what or who) than it is of operation science (which asks how).

So the positing of a designer (primary intelligent cause) of the origin of life can be a legitimate part of origin science (though not of operation science), provided that there is evidence of design (intelligent contrivance) in living organisms. Thus the task of the creationist is to provide such evidence in order to legitimate the scientific nature of its theories about origins.

Are Creationist Views Religious?

The other major objection to creationist views is that they are religious and hence ought not to be taught in the public schools. Educators offer several grounds for this conclusion. Most of them are stated or implied in the Arkansas and Louisiana court decisions. These objections fall into four major categories:

1. Creation entails a supernatural cause.
2. The concept of creation from nothing is inherently religious.
3. Teachings about creation come from a religious book (the Bible).
4. Creation implies a creator (or God).

We will examine the validity of these reasons in order.*

First, critics contend that creation entails a supernatural cause (which is religious). It is true that creation science posits a primary cause which might be supernatural. However, limiting science to a study of secondary natural causes seems unjustified for several reasons.

Historically, it is widely acknowledged that the belief in a supernatural cause played a vital role in the very origin of modern science (Gilkey 1959, 35). Indeed, for the first two-and-a-half centuries of modern science (1620–1860) most of the leading lights in science believed the universe and life gave evidence of a supernatural creator. One need only to recall names like Bacon, Kepler, Newton, Boyle,

---

*The following material first appeared in Norman L. Geisler, "Should Creation Science Be Taught in Public Schools?" NCRPE (1983).

Pascal, Mendel, Agassiz, Maxwell, and Kelvin—all of whom believed in a supernatural cause of the universe and life. This widespread belief of scientists even found its way into the foundational document of American freedom. The Declaration of Independence (1776) affirms that nature makes it "self-evident" that "all men are created. . . ."

Philosophically, it is difficult to justify an approach to origin science in which only one of the two broad categories of explanation is given a hearing. And clearly origins were by means of either primary or secondary causes. It is essential in philosophy to be open to opposing views. Furthermore, not allowing a creationist explanation of origins is contrary to present educational practice in high-school humanities and philosophy classes. Here arguments both for and against a creator are presented. The same procedure should be allowed in a science class. Keeping in mind the distinction between origin science and operation science, we only present opposing views of origins in origin science.

Scientifically, there are some serious objections to disallowing minority views. Remember Galileo. Admittedly, creation science is a minority view, but without minority views there would be no possibility of scientific progress, since all new ideas are minority views when they are first presented. By disallowing that creationist theories be presented, scientists in the name of science may be unwittingly hindering the progress of science. Of course, we agree that positing creative intervention should be permitted only in origin science, not in operation science.

Furthermore, narrowing the scope of causes to only secondary natural ones is educationally unfruitful. Some events of origin may have nonnatural primary intelligent causes. But to insist on finding a natural cause where there is evidence for primary intelligent causes is like demanding that a geology class remain at Mount Rushmore until it discovers some natural process of erosion to explain the faces formed on the mountainside.

Educationally, serious oversights are involved in forbidding the creationist view an entrance to the science classroom. With the exception of a few vocal zealots (e.g., Asimov 1981, 85), most serious-minded scientists recognize that it is at least possible that secondary-cause evolution may be false and primary-cause creation may be true. If this is so, then a court decision which forbids teaching creationist views will have the consequence of legislating the impossibility of teaching what admittedly may be true. It is difficult to believe that fair-minded scientists are willing to say in effect: "Teachings about creation may be true, but we will not allow them to be taught anyway!" Certainly we do not want to legislate against teaching the truth. At any rate, if origin science is treated as distinct from operation science, then the concern behind this objection is lessened.

Legally, to insist that only secondary natural causes can be discussed in classes dealing with origins is to unconstitutionally favor one point of view—the one represented by secondary-cause religions, such as Hinduism, Buddhism, and Secular Humanism. Secular Humanism is indeed a religion. It declared itself a religion in 1933 and the Supreme Court has noted that it is a religion protected by the First Amendment (*Torcaso v. Watkins*, 1961). But three of the essential beliefs of Secular Humanism are that there is no Creator, there was no creation, and there are no supernaturally caused events (Kurtz 1973, 8). Therefore to insist that only these points of view can be taught is to "establish" (that is, to prefer) these essential tenets of Secular Humanism in the public schools.

To be sure, these are not the only tenets of naturalistic religions, such as Secular Humanism. But if the court can declare "creation science" is religion, then there is no reason that these tenets should not be called religion when the Secular Humanists' views are presented. This is especially so when the naturalistic position on these points is the only view presented.

Second, the court ruled that teaching about creation from nothing is inherently religious. The Arkansas judge affirmed that "creation of the world 'out of nothing' is the ultimate religious statement because God is the only actor" (see Geisler 1982a, 174). But this pronouncement is a case of special pleading. For there are only two basic views on the origin of the universe: either the universe is eternal or else it came into being out of nothing. Why should we legislate that the belief in an eternal uncaused universe is not religious, but the belief that it was caused to come into existence is essentially religious? Some religions hold one of these views and other religions hold the other view. It is special pleading to call one of these two views religious and not the other.

Furthermore, if the court pronounces a view religious because it is consistent with the tenets of some religions, then most cosmological and ethical beliefs ever held by mankind are religious. Surely we do not want to forbid teaching school children that rape, murder, and cruelty are wrong simply because many religions also hold these to be wrong. Why, then, should one claim that creation is a religious teaching simply because some religions believe in it? Teaching what is compatible with certain religious beliefs is not necessarily to teach religion. Macroevolution is compatible with the beliefs of religious humanists. But teaching the scientific evidence for biological macroevolution in origin science is not necessarily to teach the religion of Secular Humanism. Likewise, simply because creationist views are compatible with certain other forms of Christian and non-Christian religions does not mean that to teach the scientific evidences for creation in origin science is to teach those religions. Neither view of origins is operation science (see appendix 2).

Third, critics charge that creation implies a creator (which is an object of religion).

At this point some object to the comparison because creation implies a creator (who is an object of worship) whereas macroevolution does not. It is true that creation implies a creator. And a creator is often an object of religious worship. However, it does not follow that positing a creator as an inference from scientific observations within the domain of origin science is thereby any more religious than not positing one.

First of all, it is now widely accepted (even by the courts) that belief or nonbelief that there is a creator (or God) is not the essential element of what is meant by religion. Indeed, the courts have consistently upheld the religious rights of atheists.* Furthermore, the simple belief that there is a creator or ultimate cause is not necessarily religious. Aristotle inferred an ultimate cause from observations about the cosmos, yet he did not worship this First Cause. The same is true of Plato's Creator; he functioned as a world Designer but not as the object of ultimate worth (that Plato reserved for the Good). Other religions (such as Gnosticism and many preliterate religions) did not perceive the creator of the universe to be an object of worship. So the concept of a first cause or creator need not be a religious one.

Furthermore, if we must eliminate any object of worship or of ultimate commitment from study in public schools, then we should also eliminate rocks from geology class because some people have worshiped rocks! Certainly all icons must be forbidden in historical or archaeological studies, for they were idols to someone. And what would this do to art classes? No Buddha and no Virgin will be allowed. All crucifixion and biblical scenes would have to be forbidden.

---

*See *Torcaso v. Watkins*, 367 U.S. 488, 81 S.Ct. 1680, 6 L.Ed. 2d 982 (1961).

As a matter of fact, most great art up to the eighteenth century has religious significance and would therefore have to be disallowed.

If the Court is right then we also must not present any historical evidence for the existence of either Buddha or Christ, for both are the object of religious devotion to millions. And presenting this evidence might have the effect of encouraging their followers to further religious devotion.

This kind of reasoning seems faulty. It is not the reference to an object which some people worship which makes it religious but whether it is presented as an object of worship or ultimate commitment. We do not forbid the study of natural forces in science classes (such as rain, wind, and sun) simply because many have worshiped these forces. We simply insist that they be studied in an objective way, without attempting to evoke a religious response or commitment to them. Indeed, we don't forbid the teaching of scientific evidence for macroevolution simply because some have made evolution into a religion. Huxley, for example, called his belief the religion of "evolutionary humanism" (1957, 181). Hence, as long as a creator is posited as a causal explanation for origins, and not an object of worship, there should be no religious objection to presenting creationist views as origin science. Likewise, Buddha and Christ can be studied from an objective historical vantage point without presenting them as objects for religious devotion. Indeed, the courts have never ruled that studies about religion or religious beings are unconstitutional. It is the teaching of religion which is considered illegal, not teaching about religion or religious objects (*Abington*, 1963).

Paul Tillich was consulted by the Supreme Court when it attempted to define what is religion (*Torcaso v. Watkins*, 1961). Tillich gave the key as to how a creator (or ultimate) may be approached in a nonreligious way. He noted that studying the ultimate from a detached, objective point of view is not religion; it is philosophy. However, when we approach the same ultimate from an involved, committed perspective this is religious. Building on Tillich's distinction, Langdon Gilkey notes that it is like two climbers scaling a mountain from different sides. They are not approaching two different peaks. There is only one ultimate. But there is more than one way this ultimate can be approached (Gilkey 1959, 35).*

*Why Gilkey did not apply his own distinction to his invalid objection that creationists are like gnostics who posit two gods (one of which is a nonreligious creator) is a mystery (see Gilkey 1982, 104).

In view of this distinction we would conclude that if one approaches a creator from the objective, detached vantage point of scientific inference he has not thereby taught religion. This is exactly what creationists propose should be done with regard to positing a creator as a possible scientific explanation of origins. But the proper domain for a creator is origin science. The idea of a cause or designer of the universe is religiously innocuous when it is presented as an explanation of origins in origin science. It is even more so when it must be presented as only one of two possible ways to explain the data. How can balanced teaching about two possible explanations in origin science be favoring or establishing one?

Fourth, critics argue that a creationist view is religious because it comes from a religious source (the Bible). One of the more curious arguments against teaching creation in origin science is the claim that it comes from a religious source, the Bible. This is a good example of the genetic fallacy.

First of all, let us suppose that the source of the idea of creation is the Bible. If this makes it religious then modern science itself can also be considered religious, for it is now widely acknowledged that the biblical doctrine of creation played a significant role in the origin of modern science. In a landmark article on this point M. B. Foster stated that without the Christian doctrine of creation there would be no modern science (1934, 448).

Second, if we must reject a scientific theory because it comes from a religious source then we must reject many archaeological discoveries. The source and inspiration of many Near-Eastern archaeological finds was the Bible. Further, we would have to reject Friedrich August Kekulé's model of the benzene molecule, since he is said to have gotten it from a vision of a snake biting its tail (Barbour 1966, 158). And we must also consider the alternating-current motor unscientific because Nikolai Tesla's idea for it came in a vision he received while he was reading a pantheistic poet (O'Neill 1980).

However, it is obviously wrong to reject a scientific model because of its source—even if the source is religious in nature. Scientists are not concerned about the source of a model but rather about its adequacy in explaining the data. Has any scholar ever rejected Socrates' philosophy simply because his inspiration for it came from a Greek prophetess? Or has any informed teacher ever refused to teach about Descartes's rationalism simply because his inspiration came from three dreams on November 10, 1619 (Maritain 1944, 13–27)?

Likewise, no fair-minded person should reject the idea of special creation simply because it comes from a religious source.

Summary and Conclusion

There are two main arguments leveled against allowing creationist views of origin to be taught in public-school science classes. It is argued that these views are not science but pseudoscience and that they are really teaching religion.

The first of these objections is based on a failure to distinguish operation science and origin science. The former is empirical science, but the latter is more like a forensic science. Operation science deals with observed regularities in the present. In this sense of the word, neither special creation nor macroevolution is science. Origin science, both special creation and macroevolution, deals with unobserved singularities in the past. So while only natural (secondary) causes are to be allowed in operation science, a primary supernatural cause is possible in origin science.

Second, to insist that primary-cause creation is religious because it is compatible or congruent with certain supernatural-cause religious beliefs (such as are found in traditional Judaism, Islam, and Christianity) is no more fair than claiming macroevolution is religious because it is compatible or congruent with beliefs of certain naturalistic-cause religions (such as Hinduism, Buddhism, and Secular Humanism). If we insist that the idea of creation should be rejected because it comes from a religious source (e.g., the Bible), then we must, for consistency's sake, also reject the idea for the benzene-molecule model or the alternating-current motor. For they too came from religious sources. If a primary cause of the origin of life is presented simply as one possible (or plausible) explanation of the origin of living things, then it has no more religious significance than teaching about natural forces or even "evolution," to which some people have given religious significance.

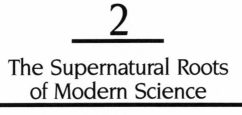

2
The Supernatural Roots of Modern Science

Theistic Background for Scientific Views

In spite of the present disfavor creationist views encounter in the scientific community, without the belief in creation there would probably have been no modern empirical science (Davis 1984, passim). It is a fact of modern history that the theistic views of early scientists vitally influenced the origin and development of modern natural science. As Alfred North Whitehead put it, "The faith in the possibility of science, generated antecedently to the development of modern scientific theory, is an unconscious derivative from medieval theology" (1925, 13). In a landmark article on this topic M. B. Foster wrote:

> The general question arises: What is the source of the un-Greek elements which were imported into philosophy by the post-Reformation philosophers, and which constitute the modernity of modern philosophy? And . . . what is the source of those un-Greek elements in the modern theory of nature by which the peculiar character of the modern science of nature was to be determined? The answer to the first question is: The Christian revelation, and the answer to the second: The Christian doctrine of creation. (1934, 448)

Foster argues that modern empirical science did not emerge from a Greek view of nature. "The modern investigators of nature were the first to take seriously *in their science* the Christian doctrine that nature is created . . ." (ibid., 453, emphasis added). As monotheists they believed the universe is upheld by the power of God (Heb. 1:3).

However, a contingent, created world is knowable by sensory experience, that is, empirically, for such a physical world is known through the physical senses. "If, therefore, the contingent is essential to nature, [then] experience must be indispensable to the science of nature" (ibid., 464). Thus by stressing the contingency of the world the Judeo-Christian doctrine of creation was an essential factor in the rise of modern empirical science.*

Unlike the Greeks, early modern scientists rejected the belief that nature is necessary and its forms (of intelligibility) eternal. For modern scientists nature is something else—it is contingent. Hence,

> the element in nature which depends upon the *voluntary* activity of God, is incapable of becoming an object to reason, and science therefore must depend, in regard to this element, upon the *evidence* of sensation. The reliance upon the senses for evidence, not merely for illustration, is what constitutes the empirical character peculiar to modern natural science; and the conclusion follows that only a created nature is proper object of an empirical science. (Ibid., 464–65, emphasis added)

Foster argues that only when the Greek concept of necessary forms in nature had given way to the Judeo-Christian idea of a contingent creation did it become necessary to take an empirical route to finding scientific truth.

According to Foster, the Greeks believed the necessary essence of nature was known by contemplation and deduction. But once theists came to view nature as a contingent creation it became necessary to use observation and experimentation to understand it. The essential difference is that for the Greeks (and medievals who followed them) the empirical was used only as an illustration of their scientific deductions, but for modern natural scientists the empirical became evidence for their scientific theories (see appendix 5).

The turning point in this change in scientific procedure came in the modern application of medieval Christian theology to the physical universe.† Medieval theologians were theists who believed that God is the supernatural cause of the natural world (cosmos). That is,

---

*Foster's general thesis has been further supported by the work of Edward B. Davis, Jr., in his dissertation (1984, at Indiana University). See pp. 178–79, 239–41.

†Theology is the study of God and his relation to his created world.

God is the primary cause who works in his world through secondary causes. According to Foster one of the reasons this supernatural, theistic view did not help to give rise to modern science earlier was that with the Reformation "philosophers claimed for reason emancipation from authority of faith, to which it had been so long submitted" (ibid., 450). The tragedy of Galileo would be a case in point. Medieval theology had been so wedded to Aristotelian science, which consisted largely of observations and deductions, that it had not perceived the inconsistency between the implications of its Christian theistic world view and its science. (The medieval Jewish scholar Moses Maimonides [*Guide for the Perplexed*] criticized Aristotle, as did Christian theists in the Middle Ages.) Once liberated from Aristotelian science, modern thinkers during the Renaissance began to draw out the logical implications of their view of creation in their approach to science, even though the unconscious influence of Aristotle had continuing results.

Furthermore, as Edward B. Davis, Jr., argues, the rise of modern empirical science was strongly influenced by scientists (like Boyle and Newton) whose Christian view of a God who freely created a contingent world manifested itself in their approach to experimental science. For "an emphasis on the divine will went hand in hand with a belief in the primacy of the phenomena." And "a lack of emphasis on the divine will was accompanied by an *a priori* attitude toward nature" which hindered empirical discoveries (Davis 1984, 236).

Most early scientists worked out their scientific views from within this theistic Christian belief in a supernatural creator and the doctrine of creation. This doctrine of creation was not a full-orbed view of origin science as it is set forth here. But neither was belief in creation simply a religious belief. Although not all early scientists were orthodox Christians, yet many believed that the physical universe gives ample evidence that its origin was the work of a supernatural creator. For others the influence was largely unconscious but real nonetheless. The list of these scientists includes the names of most of the founders of the various disciplines of modern science.

Johannes Kepler (1571–1630)	Celestial mechanics, physical astronomy
Blaise Pascal (1623–1662)	Hydrostatics
Robert Boyle (1627–1691)	Chemistry, gas dynamics

Nicolaus Steno (1638–1687)	Stratigraphy
Isaac Newton (1642–1727)	Calculus, dynamics
Michael Faraday (1791–1867)	Magnetic theory
Charles Babbage (1792–1871)	Computer science
Louis Agassiz (1807–1873)	Glacial geology, ichthyology
James Young Simpson (1811–1870)	Gynecology
Gregor Mendel (1822–1884)	Genetics
Louis Pasteur (1822–1895)	Bacteriology
William Thomson (Lord Kelvin) (1824–1907)	Energetics, thermodynamics
Joseph Lister (1827–1912)	Antiseptic surgery
James Clerk Maxwell (1831–1879)	Electrodynamics, statistical thermodynamics
William Ramsay (1852–1916)	Isotopic chemistry

The motivation to pursue the study of the natural world was the natural outworking of belief in a creator. This will become evident by more closely examining a few notable examples.

Francis Bacon (1561–1626)

Bacon's debt to the concept of creation is well known. He frankly confessed that his motivation to observe and experiment was based on the creation mandate in which God said to man: "Be fruitful and multiply, and fill the earth and subdue it; and have dominion over [it] . . ." (Gen. 1:28). Of this mandate to subdue creation Bacon wrote, "Only let the human race recover that right over nature which belongs to it by divine bequest, and let power be given it; the exercise thereof will be governed by sound reason and true religion" ([1620] 1960, 1:129:119).

Speaking of the natural world, Bacon declared, "The beginning is from God: for the business which is in hand, having the character of good so strongly impressed upon it, appears manifestly to proceed from God who is the author of good, and the Father of Lights" (ibid., 1:93:91-92). In other words, the world is good and, therefore, worthy to be studied. (The Greeks did not share this belief in the inherent goodness of the material world.) Further, the world was created by an orderly God and hence this order may be observed by his creatures.

Bacon's confidence in the need to observe and experiment is manifested in his belief that his commission is an outworking of a prophecy recorded in Daniel 12:4. He wrote:

> Nor should the prophecy of Daniel be forgotten touching the last ages of the world: 'Many shall go to and fro, and knowledge shall be increased'; clearly intimating that the thorough passage of the world (which now by so many distant voyages seems to be accomplished, or in course of accomplishment), and the advancement of the sciences, are destined by fate, that is, by Divine Providence, to meet in the same age. (Ibid., 1:93:92)

However, as is often the case with pioneers, Bacon was still influenced by previous thought and never observed and experimented much himself. Nonetheless, he made it unmistakably clear that the manifest destiny of modern science, in contrast to ancient and medieval science, was to be experimental (ibid., 1:95:93).

Bacon held that the careful observer of nature will discover "fixed laws" which he can use in subduing the world (ibid., 2:2:122). And it is this law which Bacon meant when he spoke of forms (ibid.). These "forms" (laws) are not known a priori and should not be used in "fashioning the world out of categories" (ibid., 1:63:60). Rather, they are discovered a posteriori by experience. Of course, modern science eventually softened "fixed laws" into statistical generalizations. Even so the Baconian spirit lives on in terms like "regularities," "patterns," and "types."

Bacon believed that nature, like the Bible, is the revelation of God. And Christians need not fear that any discovery in God's world (science) will destroy their faith in God's Word (Scripture). For "if the matter be truly considered, natural philosophy is, after the word of God, at once the surest medicine against superstition and the most approved nourishment for faith, and therefore she is rightly given to religion as her most faithful handmaid, since the one displays the will of God, the other his power" (ibid., 1:39:88).

So for Bacon the theistic doctrine of creation was in fact part of his stated motivation to observe the world. In this way Bacon believed he could discover the orderly laws by which God operates the world and benefits his creatures. He described three approaches to the physical universe:

> The men of experiment are like the ant, they only collect and use; the reasoners resemble spiders, who make cobwebs out of their own substance. But the bee takes a middle course: it gathers its material from the flowers of the garden and of the field, but transforms and digests it by a power of its own. (Ibid., 1:95:93)

So a modern scientist is neither a scholastic spider nor an empirical ant but a Baconian bee. He extracts from nature what is available for transformation into practical products for mankind. "For [he] neither relies solely or chiefly on the powers of the mind, nor does [he] take the matter which [he] gathers from natural history and mechanical experiments and lay it up in the memory whole, as [he] finds it, but lays it up in the understanding altered and digested" (ibid.).

Bacon's understanding of Scripture was significantly shaped by the writings of John Calvin. Both Calvin and Bacon were trained in the methods of Renaissance law. Calvin had applied this new method to Scripture, the book of God's Word. Bacon adopted this legal method of inquiry and applied it to the book of God's world. But Bacon insisted that science should not be based on passages from the Bible. He saw this error as a "vanity some of the moderns have with extreme levity indulged so far as to attempt to found a system of natural philosophy on the first chapter of Genesis, on the book of Job, and other parts of the sacred writings, seeking for the dead among the living" (ibid., 1:65:62).

Bacon replaced the old deductive method of the Aristotelians with a more inductive and experimental method. Bacon wished this new *organon* (logic) to be applied universally, for he believed that as "the common logic, which governs by the syllogisms, extends not only to natural but to all sciences, so does mine also, which proceeds by induction, embrace everything" (ibid., 1:127:116).

For Bacon true knowledge is "knowledge by causes" (ibid., 2:2:121). Traditionally there were four basic causes: the efficient cause (agent), final cause (purpose), formal cause (form), and material cause (matter). Of these causes Bacon believed "the final cause rather corrupts than advances the sciences, except such as have to do with human action" (ibid.). Likewise, "the efficient and the material (as they are investigated and received, that is, as remote causes, without reference to the latent process leading to the form) are but slight and superficial, and contribute little, if anything, to true and active science" (ibid.). This means that the proper study of empirical or operation science is the formal cause. By this Bacon did not mean a Platonic essence but the fixed laws by which the universe operates. "For though in nature nothing really exists besides individual bodies, performing pure individual acts according to a fixed law, yet in philosophy this very law, and the investigation, discovery, and explanation of it, is the foundation as well of knowledge as of operation" (ibid., 2:2:122).

Furthermore, in the domain of operation science Bacon was not concerned with the remote (primary) cause (i.e., God). He concentrated on the secondary scientific causes used by God in the operation of the universe (ibid., 2:2:121). With these new emphases Bacon gave fresh direction for modern science. Bacon did not invent the distinction between a primary and secondary cause. This he inherited from his medieval predecessors (see Thomas Aquinas, *Summa theologica* 1a.104.2). But when the distinction was applied to nature by early scientists, scientific efforts were directed to finding secondary causes for how the universe operates. So even though modern science grew out of a belief in a theistic (primary) cause, nonetheless its preoccupation became an understanding of how God works in his creation through secondary causes.

Johannes Kepler (1571–1630)

Kepler's astronomical views were also bedded deeply in his theistic beliefs about creation and the Creator. Many think of Kepler as a kind of Pythagorean mystic. But Kepler reveals his self-conscious roots in an early letter:

> May God make it come to pass that my delightful speculation [the *Mysterium Cosmographicum*] have everywhere among reasonable men fully the effect which I strove to obtain in the publication; namely, that the belief in the creation of the world be fortified through this external support, that thought of the creator be recognized in its nature, and that his inexhaustible wisdom shine forth daily more brightly. Then man will at last measure the power of his mind on the true scale, and

will realize that *God, who founded everything in the world according to the norm
of quantity, also has endowed man with a mind which can comprehend these norms.*
(Cited by Holton 1973, 84, emphasis added)

In other words, Kepler believed that God created the world to
operate in a regular and orderly way (mathematically) so that we may,
by observing these natural laws, think God's thoughts after him. For
"those laws [which govern the material world] lie within the power of
understanding of the human mind; God wanted us to perceive them
when he created us in His image in order that we may take part of His
own thoughts. . . ." And "our knowledge [of numbers and quantities]
is of the same kind as God's, at least insofar as we can understand
something of it in this mortal life" (ibid., 85). So for Kepler, to study
nature is to study the mind of God.

Kepler viewed the universe as a great mathematical machine created by God. Thus he wrote,

My aim in this is to show that the celestial machine is to be likened not
to a divine organism but rather to a clockwork . . . , insofar as nearly all
the manifold movements are carried out by means of a single, quite
simple magnetic force, as in the case of a clockwork all motions [are
caused] by a simple weight. Moreover I show how this physical conception is to be presented through calculation and geometry. (Ibid., 72)

It is in view of this mathematical regularity that Kepler believed
one could study the universe in a scientific way. However, the Greeks
(particularly Pythagoras) believed this as well, as least about the
moon. However, Kepler was not a Pythagorean but a Christian using
Pythagorean math as a tool to express his Christian belief that the
universe behaved like a machine which he believed was created by
God. Pythagoreans did not deny, as Kepler did, that the world is a
giant organism. What was unique about Kepler's view was his Christian belief that since the physical universe is a creation of God, then
one can discover something about ultimate reality (God) through
observing the real physical world.

For Kepler the physical world is not only real but observation of it
is the basis on which we correct any a priori mathematical speculation about it.

My aim is to assume only those things of which I do not doubt they are
real and consequently physical, where one must refer to the nature of

the heavens, not the elements. When I dismiss the perfect eccentric and the epicycle, I do so because they are purely geometrical assumptions, for which a corresponding body in the heavens does not exist. (Ibid., 78)

It was because of this that Kepler rejected his own theory that disagreed with Tycho Brahe's data regarding eight minutes of arc in the orbit of Mars. In short, Kepler's scientific approach to reality can be stated as follows: "The physically real world, which defines the nature of things, is the world of phenomena explainable by mechanical principles" (ibid., 78).

Kepler assumed (as the Pythagoreans did) that the universe was mathematically analyzable. But unlike the Greeks, Kepler believed that since the observable physical world was a creation of God, one could come to know God's thoughts by studying the physical laws of the universe. Hence Kepler was a pioneer in applying the laws of physics to astronomy. He claimed that "from these magnetic [gravitational] forces, by other propositions which are also mathematical, I deduce the motions of the planets, the comets, the moon, and the sea." Kepler also desired to "derive the rest of the phenomena of nature by the same kind of reasoning from mechanical principles . . ." (ibid., 77). The genius of Kepler's view was not that God was the solution of some scientific problem but that without a creator of the physical world there could be no operation science. So to leave the Creator out, as the Greeks did, is to deify nature and frustrate the efforts to have a true science of nature.

Writing to the German astronomer David Fabricius (1564–1617), Kepler said, "the difference consists only in this, that you use circles, I use bodily forces" (Aug. 1, 1607; ibid., 77). Even Kepler's former teacher, Michael Mastlin, tried to dissuade him, saying,

Concerning the motion of the moon you write you have traced all the inequalities to physical causes; I do not quite understand this. I think rather that here one should leave physical causes out of account, and should explain astronomical matters only according to astronomical method with the aid of astronomical, not physical, causes and hypotheses. That is, the calculation demands astronomical bases in the field of geometry and arithmetic. . . . (Ibid., 76)

Kepler was convinced that the Creator had left his imprint on his physical creation in a distinct way; he was also convinced that it was worth his while giving up the Christian ministry (for which he had prepared) to pursue his scientific inquiries. He wrote, "I wanted to become a theologian; for a long time I was restless: Now, however, observe how through my efforts God is being celebrated in astronomy" (ibid., 86). In brief, Kepler's revolutionary discoveries in science were grounded in his belief that the universe is a finite, contingent creation of God. His theistic beliefs were a strong influence on his approach to nature and made his scientific views characteristically modern. His belief (like Bacon's) in a primary cause (God), who worked in his creation in an orderly way, formed the basis of his study of the secondary causes in the world of nature.

Galileo Galilei (1564–1642)

It is known that Nicolaus Copernicus had rejected Ptolemaic astronomy (c. 1507). However, it is well known that Copernicus did little observation or experimentation. In fact, his desire to change the Ptolemaic system was more aesthetic and mathematical than empirical (Butterfield [1951] 1957, chap. 2). For Galileo this was not the case.

Galileo believed "the Holy Scriptures and Nature are both produced by the Word of God; the former is the result of the dictation of the Holy Spirit, and the latter is the most obedient agent of the ordinances of God" ([1615] 1965, 8). Furthermore, said Galileo, "I do not believe the same God who gave us our senses, our reason and our intellect intended that we should neglect these gifts and the information they give us about nature, or that we should deny what our senses and our reason have observed by experiment or logical demonstration . . ." (ibid., 9). Hence, "to forbid science completely would mean condemning hundreds of passages of the Holy Scriptures that teach us how the glory and greatness of God are marvelously discovered in all of his works, and how things about God are to be read in the open book of the sky" (ibid., 20). Indeed, one such biblical passage reads, "The heavens are telling the glory of God; and the firmament proclaims his handiwork" (Ps. 19:1).

Galileo was strongly opposed to interpreting the Bible literalistically in contradiction to the findings of valid scientific observations and inferences. He believed "it is the intention of the Holy Spirit [in Scripture] to teach us how one goes to heaven, and not how the heavens go" (ibid., 11). Hence it is clear that "the Holy Spirit did not intend to teach us whether the sky moves or stands still, or whether it is in the shape of a disc or a plane, or whether the earth is contained in the center or set off at one side" (ibid., 10). These are all matters left for discovery by scientists. In fact, said Galileo, "the Holy Spirit has purposely refrained from instructing us in such propositions, because they are in no way related to his intention, which is our salvation" (ibid., 11).

The cause of theological disapproval of science Galileo identified as a biblical literalism which assumes that if the Bible says "the sun stood still" (Josh. 10:13) that in fact the universe is geocentric and Copernicus was wrong. Although this is disputed, even the great Reformer Martin Luther is (mis?)quoted as saying of Copernicus,

> whoever wants to be clever must agree with nothing that others esteem. He must do something of his own. This is what that fellow |Copernicus| does who wishes to turn the whole of astronomy upside down. Even in these things that are thrown into disorder I believe the Holy Scriptures, for Joshua commanded the sun to stand still and not the earth. (Luther |June 4, 1539| 1967)

In contradistinction to this kind of view Galileo asks, "Now who would insist that, in making incidental references to earth, water, sun or other created things, the Scriptures must rigorously adhere to the most simple and literal meaning of the words?" (|1615| 1965, 7). In other words, one must not take the Bible literally here, but one must take science more seriously.

Quoting Copernicus, Galileo noted that the learned Lactantius even "ridiculed those who taught that the earth was a sphere" (ibid., 5). Such people require that "in purely scientific matters that have nothing to do with religion, one should abandon completely the use of his senses and all conclusions based upon evidence, on the strength of some random quotation of Scripture which seems to be contradictory even though the clear teaching is about another subject" (ibid.).

In astronomy or any field of science, Galileo believed, the multiplicity of facts leads to the discovery, growth, and stability of the sciences. These facts are discovered "by clear experiments and scientific proofs" (ibid., 4, 5). Hence, "our discussions about natural and scientific matters should not begin with the authority of Scripture passages, but with physical experiments and logical proofs" (ibid., 8).

For "when we learn things about natural phenomena by experimental observation or by logical demonstration, these things should not be called into doubt or condemned because the wording of Scripture texts seems to contradict them" (ibid.).

Furthermore, if we use authority to forbid belief in the realm of operation science,

> we would have to forbid men to look toward the heavens and to notice how Mars and Venus can be 60 times and 40 times brighter and larger at one season than at another, or to notice how the same Venus is sometimes round and at other times hooked with very thin horns, or to notice many other facts that cannot possibly be explained by the Ptolemaic system, but are convincing arguments for the Copernican system. (Ibid., 19)

But scientific observations cannot and should not be stopped, nor should religious authority be positioned against them.

Galileo's theistic beliefs, like those of other early scientists, provided an implicit conviction that God had created regular and discoverable laws by which the universe operated. In fact, "all of the verses of Scripture are not obliged to function as rigorously as every law of nature. And it is no less excellent to discover the works of God in nature than in the sayings of Holy Scripture" (ibid., 8).

Galileo further noted that

> if they think carefully about the binding force of clear deductions, they may recognize how it is impossible for professors of the experimental sciences to change their opinions at will. They simply cannot turn away from one thing and turn toward another. There is a great difference between commanding a mathematician or a scientist and directing a merchant or a lawyer. You simply cannot change the experimental conclusions about natural phenomena and the heavens, as you can alter the terms of a contract, revise the interest rate or change a business deal. (Ibid., 17)

Why is this so? Because, said Galileo, the observable laws of nature operate with unalterable regularity. Theories must fit nature; nature cannot be changed to fit our theories. God works in regular ways in the operation of his universe.

Galileo recognized that not all things in science could be proved conclusively. Nonetheless, he was firmly convinced that the laws of nature are so regular that with proper observation, experimentation, and deductions one could confirm hypotheses beyond reasonable doubt (ibid., 18). The operational laws of the universe are regular and available for testing.

Galileo believed that the operation of the natural world is available for scientific scrutiny, but "matters of faith concerning supernatural things . . . are to be believed by faith" (ibid., 17). The supernatural is the source of the natural world, but the natural is the proper domain of science. Science deals with "natural phenomena" (ibid., 17) which can be observed and with which one can perform experiments. The supernatural realm is not subject to such test. Thus, mere ignorance of natural causes of the operation of the world is not a sufficient justification for positing a supernatural cause. In matters of natural science "the first question to be determined is whether they have been clearly demonstrated by observed evidence, or whether it is possible to arrive at such evidence and demonstrations" (ibid., 22). Such scientific conclusions were God-given, said Galileo, because

> I do not believe that the same God who gave us our senses, our reason and our intellect intended that we should neglect these gifts and the information they give us about nature, or that we should deny what our senses and our reason have observed by experiment or logical demonstration, while providing for ourselves other sources of information. (Ibid., 9)

In short, for Galileo there were two great spheres of God's truth: one in Scripture and one in nature. Galileo believed these two realms do not contradict each other nor do they trespass on each other's territory. Hence, what can be demonstrated by observation and experimentation takes precedence over any literalistic interpretation of the Bible to the contrary. By this distinction Galileo hoped to secure the domain of operation science from unjustified intrusions by religious dogma while retaining nonetheless his belief in a supernatural origin of the natural world.

Galileo's motive for studying the cosmos was to discover the message the Creator is proclaiming therein. In using the God-given faculties of reason to observe and experiment with nature one is merely fulfilling the Creator's mandate. Hence, for Galileo too his theistic belief in the primary cause (Creator) of the world prompted his scientific study of the secondary causes of the natural world.

Isaac Newton (1642–1727)

Another giant among the founding fathers of modern science was Isaac Newton. His formulation of the laws of gravity was paradigmatic for much of science to follow. Newton admitted Kepler's influence on him, saying, "I gathered it from Kepler's theories about twenty years ago" (July 14, 1685; Holton 1973, 89). Like Kepler before him, Newton believed that God created the solar system. He held that the entire solar system was formed from a "common chaos" which is described in Genesis 1:2. From this chaos the "spirit of God," by means of gravitational attraction, formed the separate planets (Numbers 1977, 5).

Although Newton believed natural laws were used as an instrumental cause in creation, he was emphatic in his contention that it is necessary to posit God as the efficient primary cause of the universe. In a letter to Thomas Burnet he insisted that "where natural causes are at hand God uses them as instruments in his works, but I do not think them alone sufficient for ye creation . . ." (ibid., 4).

Newton contended that the orderly patterns in the planets resulted from a primary cause, or creator. For

it is not to be conceived that mere mechanical causes could give birth to so many regular motions, since the comets range over all parts of the heavens in very eccentric orbits; for by that kind of motion they pass easily through the orbs of the planets, and with great rapidity; and in their aphelions, where they move the slowest, and are detained the longest, they recede to the greatest distances from each other, and hence suffer the least disturbance from their mutual attractions. This most beautiful system of the sun, planets, and comets, could only proceed from the counsel and dominion of an intelligent and powerful Being. ([1687] 1952, 369)

The concept of God held by Newton was more Judeo-Christian (theistic) than Greek in nature. For him "this Being governs all things, not as the soul of the world, but as Lord over all; and on account of his dominion he is wont to be called Lord God or Universal Ruler." For "Deity is the dominion of God not over his own body, as those imagine who fancy God to be the soul of the world, but over servants. The Supreme God is a Being eternal, infinite, absolutely perfect" (ibid., 370).

Newton goes on to describe this Creator as "the God of Israel, the God of Gods." He is a God with dominion over all creation.

And from his true dominion it follows that the true God is a living, intelligent, and powerful Being; and, from his other perfections, that he is supreme, or most perfect. He is eternal and infinite, omnipotent and omniscient; that is, his duration reaches from eternity to eternity; his presence from infinity to infinity; he governs all things, and knows all things that are or can be done. (Ibid., 370)

This Judeo-Christian concept of God was at the very center of Newton's cosmology. Indeed, like that of the other early scientists, Newton's belief in theistic creation lay at the very foundation of his whole scientific enterprise. The universe was God's great machine, and the scientist could discover the laws by which this machine operates— the laws of God. Thus for Newton God is the primary cause of the universe and natural laws are the secondary causes by which God operates in the natural world.

Summary and Conclusion

Early modern scientific approaches to the operation of the universe, in contrast to Greek views, sprang out of a belief that the cosmos was freely created by God and that he works in it in a regular way. Indeed, the earliest scientists, whose works are foundational to modern scientific methodology, were themselves inspired and directed by these creationist beliefs. Langdon Gilkey summarized the situation well when he wrote,

The religious idea of a transcendent Creator actually made possible rather than hindered the progress of the scientific understanding of the natural order. In a real sense the modern conviction that existence is good because it is intelligible to scientific inquiry finds some of its most significant roots in the Christian belief that God created the world. (1959, 110)*

There is, however, a bitter irony in this for creationists. The very scientific method which was fostered by a belief in a creator and his creation was, within two centuries, to be used to replace creationist

*Quotes like this make it even more difficult to understand Gilkey's more recent opposition to the scientific validity of creationists' beliefs (see Gilkey 1985, passim).

beliefs about origins. Early scientists shifted the emphasis from the primary cause (God) to the secondary causes (natural laws) through which he operates in the natural world. And by its subsequent preoccupation with these secondary causes, science eventually came to reject the legitimacy of positing a primary cause for these origin events. In short, natural science came to bite the supernatural hand that fed it.

3

The Emergence of a Modern Naturalistic Approach to Origins in Astronomy

During three centuries of scientific development after the time of Nicolaus Copernicus (d. 1543), a scientific consciousness arose in English and Continental society. This new awareness held that scientific knowledge of the operations of the world is acquired by observation and experimentation (see chap. 2). By the late nineteenth century the attitude was summarized by the London *Times* (Sept. 19, 1870): "We look to men of science rather for observation than for imagination." Gradually the study of the operational laws of the universe was extended farther and farther back until it included origins. In this way the role of a primary (supernatural) cause of the various origin events was gradually squeezed out of a scientific study of the past. In effect, secondary (natural) causes could account for origins, and there was no need to suppose that a primary cause had intervened. At least so most of the scientific establishment came to believe. In this manner the domain of origin science (such as cosmogony) was taken over by operation science (cosmology).

The emerging principles for the study of the universe were borrowed from physics and applied first in the area of astronomy. Several names stand out: Descartes, Buffon, Kant, and Laplace. Later these scientific principles were applied to geology and biology. Here three names loom large: Hutton and Lyell in geology, and Darwin in biology.

René Descartes (1596–1650)

Descartes was fearful of publishing his thoughts on science when he heard of Galileo's experiences. Galileo was denounced from the pulpit in Florence (1614) for propounding heretical (Copernican) views in his *Letters on the Solar System* (1613). Later, the Holy Office in Rome (1616) condemned his Copernican views. After he published his *Dialogue on the Two Principal Systems of the World* (1632) the Inquisition forced him to renounce his heliocentric beliefs and to retire. In spite of Galileo's fate, eventually Descartes cautiously and hypothetically set forth his views on scientific method in his *Discourse on Method* (1637).

Descartes described his scientific task: "I first tried to discover the general principles or first causes of all that exists or could exist in the world, without taking any causes into consideration but God as creator, and without using any evidence save certain indications of the truth which we find in our own minds." ([1637] 1956, 41).

It seems clear from this quotation that Descartes's "first causes" were really secondary causes or "general principles" (laws) by which God operates in his universe. In this way he elevated secondary causes (natural explanation) to the sphere once reserved by theists for a primary cause (the supernatural). In effect, operation science had crowded out origin science.

Although Descartes's general approach to nature was deductive, he found that this deductive approach would go only so far. For he discovered that it was "impossible for the human mind to distinguish the forms or species of objects found on earth from an infinity of others which might have been there if God had so willed." In view of this, Descartes recognized that it was impossible to proceed further deductively. Thus he concluded that "if we were to understand and make use of things, we would have to discover causes by their effects, and make use of many experiments" (ibid., 41). Science, then, involves finding the natural causes of observed effects. For "the truth of the hypothesis is proved by the actuality of the effects" (ibid., 49).

Descartes recognized there is an "infinite number of experiments" (ibid., 48) to perform in science. The need for these experiments is prompted by "careful observations" (ibid., 33) on which science is based. These observational experiments are necessary in order to find the proper cause of recurring events in the natural world. Descartes confessed, "My greatest difficulty usually is to find which of these is the true explanation, and to do this I know no other way than to seek several experiments such that their outcomes would be different according to the choice of hypotheses" (ibid., 41–42).

Descartes believed "the rules of mechanics . . . are the same as the rules of nature . . ." (ibid., 35). He believed to "have also discovered certain laws which God has so established in nature, and the notion of which he has so fixed in our minds, that after sufficient reflection we cannot doubt that they are exactly observed in all which exists or which happens in the world" (ibid., 26–27). These laws Descartes believed were universal, for "nature is such that even if God had created several worlds, there would have been none where these laws were not observed" (ibid., 28).

Remembering Galileo's fate, Descartes was careful to apply his naturalistic approach to origins only hypothetically (which religious authorities allowed). After stating his belief that God created the world in a completed form, he speculated as to how God could have chosen to create through purely natural processes (i.e., secondary causes). But he elected to "speak only of what would happen in a new [world], if God should now create, somewhere in imaginary space, enough matter to make one" (ibid., 27). God would need only to agitate "the various parts of this matter without order, making a chaos as confused as the poets could imagine, but . . . afterward [do] nothing but lend his usual support to nature, allowing it to behave according to the laws he had established" (ibid., 27).

Descartes added, however, that "there were no phenomena of this world which would not or at least could not occur similarly in the world [he] was describing" (ibid., 28). It was only a matter of time before scientists would apply this naturalistic approach to the actual world and not just to a hypothetical one. In this way a primary (supernatural) cause would be replaced by secondary causes; supernatural activity would be explained by natural causality.

As to how this process would apply to living things Descartes admitted ignorance, saying, "But I did not as yet know enough to speak of these in the same style as of the rest, in showing the causes of their existence and showing from what origin and in what manner nature must have produced them." As a result, he added, "I was therefore satisfied to assume that God formed the body of a man just like our own, both in the external configuration of its members and in the internal configuration of its organs, without using in its composition any matter but that which I had described" (ibid., 29).

Some scholars believe that Descartes already accepted a cautious evolutionary viewpoint. Bentley Glass argues that although Descartes

> spoke in veiled terms of the living inhabitants of his mechanistic universe, no one who reads carefully the fifth part of the *Discourse on Method* will be left with much doubt that inwardly he firmly believed that plants and animals were part of the natural order—and in consequence the product of a gradual evolution produced by the uninterrupted operation of purely physical causes. (Glass 1959, 37)

It was only a matter of time before others would explicitly apply the principles Descartes used in cosmology and physics to the realms of geology and biology.

Descartes had little scientific concern for final causes (why the world operates as it does). He described science as a search for how things operate:

> Thence I went on to speak particularly of the earth: *how*, even though I had expressly supposed that God had given no weight to the matter of which it was composed, all its parts would tend exactly toward its center; *how* the disposition of the celestial bodies and stars, principally the moon, would cause an ebb and flow in the water and air on its surface, similar in all respects to the tides of our seas, and in addition a certain current, as much of water as of air, from east to west, such as we find in the tropics; *how* mountains, seas, springs and rivers could naturally occur, metals come to be in mines, plants grow in the fields, and, in general, *how* the whole genus of mixed or composite objects would be formed. ([1637] 1956, 28, emphasis added)

The desire to know how the universe operates extended to the earthly bodies as well. Descartes said, "Since outside of the stars I knew nothing but fire which produced light, I strove to explain quite clearly the whole of the nature of fire; how it is produced and maintained; how sometimes it has heat without light and sometimes light without heat." With glee he added, "I found a particular pleasure in describing it" (ibid., 29). But the zeal to know how overrode the desire to know who; the passion to know about secondary causes overshadowed the need to posit a primary cause in science. In short, considerations about the primary cause (God) were left to the realm of philosophy and theology. The preoccupation of science was with the operation of the universe, not with its ultimate origin. Cosmology was replacing cosmogony in science. Science was to be concerned only with the secondary causes by which the universe is operated, not any ultimate primary cause by which it originated.

According to Descartes, the scientific method is not limited to the physical universe. "What pleased me most about this method," he said, "was that it enabled me to reason in all things, if not perfectly, at least as well as was in my power" (ibid., 14). That is, it was a method for approaching not only science but philosophy as well. This being the case it seemed inevitable that someone would eventually eliminate consideration of primary causality from the metaphysical realm as Descartes had in theory removed it from the physical or scientific realm.

Descartes envisioned a practical benefit for mankind through the scientific method, in contrast to the scholastic philosophy he was taught in the schools. As soon as he had achieved some general notions about physics and tested them in various critical problems he said, "I noticed how far they might lead and how they differed from the principles accepted up to this time. I thought that I could not keep them hidden without gravely sinning against the rule that obliges us to promote as far as possible the general good of mankind" (ibid., 39–40).

Descartes enumerated four rules for his newfound scientific approach to the world:

> The first rule was never to accept anything as true unless I recognized it to be evidently such. . . . The second was to divide each of the difficulties which I encountered into as many parts as possible, and as might be required for an easier solution. The third was to think in an orderly fashion, beginning with the things which were simplest and easiest to understand, and gradually and by degrees reaching toward more complex knowledge. . . . The last was always to make enumerations so complete, and reviews so general, that I would be certain that nothing was omitted. (Ibid., 12)

Armed with these principles, employing repeated observations of nature, and utilizing as many experiments as possible, Descartes wrote a new chapter in modern science. For by the discovery of natural causes he envisioned that practical applications for the benefit of mankind could and would be made. All of this he did without invoking any supernatural (primary) cause for the origin of living things. His scientific concern was with how (secondary causes), not with who (primary cause) or why (final cause).

Georges Louis Leclerc de Buffon (1707–1788)

Buffon believed that the universe is "regulated by such an amazing display of power and intelligence" that it points to "an all-potent and wonderful creator" (1797, 5). However, he hastened to add that "the various generation of men, animals, and plants, succeed each other without interruption; the earth produces fully sufficient for their subsistence; the sea has its limits; its motion and the currents of air are regulated by fixed laws" (ibid., 6). Furthermore, for the scientist,

> it should be remembered that it is an historian's business to describe, not invent; that no suppositions should be admitted upon subjects that depend upon facts and observation; that his imagination ought only to be exercised for the purpose of combining observations, rendering facts more general, and forming one connected whole, so as to present to the mind a distinct arrangement of clear ideas and probable conjectures. (Ibid., 4–5)

Buffon was opposed to invoking "remote causes" (primary causes) to explain natural events, because "such causes would produce any effects we chose, and from a single hypothesis of their nature, a thousand physical romances might be drawn, and which the authors might term, THE THEORY OF THE EARTH" (ibid., 39). These he dismissed as "vain speculations" and "mere possibilities" and added:

> but to preserve consistency, we must take the earth as it is, closely observing every part, and by inductions judge of the future from what exists at present; in other respects we ought not to be affected by causes which seldom happen, and whose effects are always sudden and violent; they do not occur in the common course of nature; but effects which are daily repeated, motions which succeed each other without interruption, and operations that are constant, ought alone to be the grounds of our reasoning. (Ibid., 40)

On the basis of his search for purely natural (secondary) causes Buffon rejected Noah's deluge as the explanation of the earth's geological column. He wrote:

> Now I insist that these strata must have been formed by degrees, and not all at once, by any revolution |catastrophe| whatever, because strata, composed of heavy materials, are very frequently found placed above light ones, which could not be, if, as some authors assert, the whole had been mixed with the water at the time of the Deluge, and afterwards precipitated. (Ibid., 18)

Buffon saw a constancy of natural law "from the creation" (ibid., 20). Rather than posit causes for "sudden and violent" effects, he held that "effects which are daily repeated, motions which succeed each other without interruption, and operations that are constant, ought alone to be the grounds of our reasoning" (ibid., 40).

These same principles were applied to the solar system. Buffon wrote that "the systematic order of the universe is laid open to the eyes of all those who can distinguish truth from error" (ibid., 73). Thus he concluded:

> We evidently see that the force of attraction always drawing the planets toward the sun, they would fall in a perpendicular line, on that planet, if they were not repelled by some other power that obliges them to move in a straight line, and which impulsive force would compel them to fly off the tangents of their respective orbits, if the force of attraction ceased one moment. (Ibid., 73–74)

Although Buffon believed "the force of impulsion was certainly communicated to the planets by the hand of the Almighty when he gave motion to the universe," yet he hastened to add:

> but as we ought as much as possible to abstain in physics from having recourse to supernatural causes, it appears that a probable reason may be given for this impulsive force, perfectly accordant with the law of mechanics, and not by any means more astonishing than the changes and revolutions which may and must happen in the universe. (Ibid., 74)

So like others of his time Buffon shifted the emphasis from the origin to the operation of the universe; from the primary cause to the study of secondary (natural) causes. The role of the supernatural was squeezed out of the natural world.

Immanuel Kant (1724–1804)

Kant confessed to being awakened from his "dogmatic slumbers" by David Hume, who also influenced James Hutton's naturalistic views in geology. From Hume he gained arguments against both rationalistic and supernaturalistic approaches to the world. Having given up on man's ability to know reality in itself, Kant contented himself with a knowledge of the phenomena, or the natural world as it appeared to him.

In the observable, knowable realm of nature Kant was impressed with the Newtonian law of gravitation. It seemed to him to be an example of a universally true law about the empirical world. This became for Kant the ideal for all science—to discover universal laws by which one could understand the universe.

Kant believed that "the investigation of nature takes its own independent course, keeping the chain of natural causes in conformity with universal laws" ([1781] 1965, 564). He was quick to add that these universal laws "proceed in accordance with the idea of an author of the universe . . ." (ibid.). But the laws so established are regulative of the entire physical universe. The scientist can allow no exceptions to them.

Although Kant did not deny the existence of a supernatural Creator, he did insist that the scientist not use the supernatural as part of his scientific understanding of the world. In fact, he argued against miraculous intervention, insisting that no one "will assert that this [amazing system of nature] is a mere result of natural laws; no one, indeed, can claim to *comprehend* whether or not the direct influence of the Creator is required on each occasion." Since, however, we do "experience all these things[,] they are *for us*, therefore, nothing but natural effects and *ought* never to be adjudged otherwise; for such [a distinction] the modesty of reason demands in its pronouncements." But "to venture beyond these limits is rashness and immodesty, although those who support miracles frequently pretend to exhibit a humble and self-renouncing way of thought" ([1793] 1960, 84, emphasis added).

Why must natural causes be assumed for all events in the natural world? Because science seeks natural laws and natural laws are universal. If we admit the supernatural into science, these "miracles must be admitted as [occurring] *daily* (though indeed hidden under the guise of natural events) or else *never*, . . ." but "in the latter case they underlie neither our explanations by reason nor the guiding rules of our conduct. . . ." And "since the former alternative [that they occur daily] is not at all compatible with reason, nothing remains but to adopt the latter maxim—for this principle remains ever a mere maxim for making judgments, not a theoretical assertion" (ibid., emphasis added).

In short, in science "we can determine nothing on the basis of knowledge of the object (which, by our own admission, transcends our understanding) but only on the basis of the maxims which are necessary to the use of our reason" (ibid.). For

> if instead of looking for causes in the universal laws of material mechanism, we appeal directly to the unsearchable decree of supreme wisdom . . . we have merely dispensed with [reason's] employment—an employment which is wholly dependent for guidance upon the order of nature and the series of its alterations, in accordance with the universal laws which they are found to exhibit. (Kant [1781] 1965, 562)

Thus science deals with natural laws, and natural laws are universal. But miracles are exceptions. Hence, for Kant, science as science cannot admit the possibility of supernatural intervention into the world.

Kant did not deny that miracles are theoretically possible or that supernatural events may ever occur. He simply noted that they do not come under the domain of science because science deals with the universal laws which regulate the world. Scientific laws are not to be thought of "as *constitutive* principles for the extension of our knowledge to more objects than experience can give but as *regulative* principles of the systematic unity of the manifold of empirical knowledge in general . . ." (ibid., 550, emphasis added). Ideas such as "world" (cosmos) are only "a schema of the regulative principle of the systematic unit of all knowledge of nature" (ibid., 552). In short, if we are going to have a cosmology it will be possible only through universal principles which regulate our knowledge of the whole cosmos.

Kant was one of the first thinkers in the modern world to apply scientific principles to speculation about the origin of the solar system. In short, he believed we must assume that the universal principles (secondary causes) that regulate the world today also did so in the past. Thus secondary causes were extended from observation of the operation of the universe to questions of origin. Without this methodology Kant believed there would be no possibility of a science about the past. His own nebular hypothesis preceded those of both Georges Louis Leclerc de Buffon and Pierre Simon de Laplace. For Kant, interjecting the supernatural into a scientific explanation of origins is a false form of "physico-theology" (ibid., 562). A creator should not be used as a factor in a purely scientific explanation of origins. This is not to deny the existence of God but simply to note that the concept has no scientific significance, whatever religious significance it may have.

Like most other thinkers of his time Kant embraced the principle of continuity in nature. He believed that

> human nature occupies as it were the middle rung of the Scale of Being, . . . equally removed from the two extremes. If the contemplation of the most sublime classes of rational creatures, which inhabit Jupiter or Saturn, arouses his envy and humiliates him with a sense of his own inferiority, he may again find contentment and satisfaction by turning his gaze upon those lower grades which, in the planets Venus and Mercury, are far below the perfection of human nature. (Cited by Lovejoy [1936] 1960, 193)

When Kant spelled out his nebular hypothesis of cosmic evolution he was, as Arthur O. Lovejoy noted, "simply giving a temporalized version of the principle of plentitude [or continuity]" (ibid., 265).

Kant's nebular hypothesis is a clear example of how physical laws were applied to the study of origins, of how the natural laws of physics were applied to cosmogony. The seeds of Kant's views are in an essay (1754) in which he argued that observation in the present is the key to the past, that is, the principle of uniformity (Ley 1968, xii–xiii). Unfortunately for him, Kant's book was impounded when his printer went out of business and it was not until 1763 that he condensed his original ideas in *The Only Possible Argument for a Demonstration of the Existence of God*. In this work Kant anticipated Laplace's *Celestial Mechanics* (1799) by a generation.

Kant stated that his purpose was "to discover the system which binds together the great members of the creation in the whole extent of infinitude, and to derive the formation of the heavenly bodies themselves, and the origin of their movements, from the primitive state of nature by mechanical laws, seems to go far beyond the power of human reason" ([1755] 1968, 5). He recognized the similarities of his views with those of the ancient materialists Leucippus and Democritus. However, Kant offered this olive branch to those still concerned about a primary cause: "I find matter bound to certain necessary laws. Out of its universal dissolution and dissipation I see a beautiful and orderly whole quite naturally developing itself. This does not take place by accident, or of chance; but it is perceived that natural qualities necessarily bring it about" (ibid., 13–14).

In brief, Kant's naturalistic explanation of origins went like this: God created matter and endowed it with certain characteristics which would unfold into the whole physical and living universe in accordance with universal, mechanical laws such as the laws of attraction and repulsion elaborated by Newton. Kant accepted "the matter of the whole world at the beginning as in a state of general dispersion, . . . a complete chaos." He added, "I see this matter forming itself in accordance with the established laws of attraction, and modifying its movement by repulsion" (ibid., 11). Thus the role of a primary cause was left only for those who saw a need to posit a first cause of the material universe.

Kant rejected any discontinuities in the evolutionary unfolding of the universe from pure matter. He labeled these "arbitrary hypotheses" (ibid., 11) and disdained any attempt to suppose that God intervened after the initial creation of matter. It seemed to Kant that "we can here say with intelligent certainty and without audacity: 'Give me matter, and I will construct a world out of it!' i.e. give me matter and I will show you how a world shall arise out of it" (emphasis added). For "if we have matter existing endowed with an essential force of attraction, it is not difficult to determine those causes which may have contributed to the arrangement of the system of the world as a whole" (ibid., 17).

But what about the question "Are we in a position to say: 'Give me matter and I will show you how a caterpillar can be produced?'" (ibid., 17). Kant's answer was indeed a bold assertion for his day. However, he did modify his anticipation of an eventual naturalistic explanation for the origin of living things by adding, "The cause of their movements, and, in short, the origin of the whole present constitution of the universe, will become intelligible before the production of a single herb or a caterpillar by mechanical causes, will become distinctly and completely understood" (ibid., 17).

From whence did Kant receive this confidence that a natural explanation for the origin of everything in the universe would ultimately be discovered? Kant responded: "These are the grounds on which I base my confidence that the physical part of universal science may hope in the future to reach the same perfection as that to which Newton has raised the mathematical half of it" (ibid., 18). As Newton had discovered physical laws with mathematical certainty, even so Kant believed these same laws were expressed in astronomy, geology, and even biology. Kant realized that he could not demonstrate the existence of such laws. He admitted his reasoning was based on "analogies and harmonies, which are in accordance with the rules of credibility and correct reasoning, . . ." but no more (ibid., 24). Nonetheless, Kant believed such laws existed and would be discovered eventually.

For those orthodox members of the religious community who believed his thoroughgoing naturalism in science was tantamount to atheism, Kant offered these words of consolation: "There is a God, just because nature even in chaos cannot proceed otherwise than regularly and according to order" (ibid., 14). That is to say, the very fact that matter unfolds in such an orderly way shows there must have been a God who thus ordered matter. But science is the study of the orderly development of matter and does not recognize divine interruptions.

Pierre Simon de Laplace (1749–1827)

Laplace denied having read about Kant's nebular hypothesis before he developed his own similar cosmogony. In any event, Laplace made his own contribution to the development of a scientific approach to origins by extending the application of natural (secondary) causes to everything, including astronomical origins. In short, for Laplace science has no room for a primary cause.

Like Francis Bacon, Laplace believed that "hypotheses founded upon facts and rectified continually by new observations . . . are the principal means for arriving at truth" ([1814] 1951, 176). He says "the surest method which can guide us in the search for truth, consists in rising by induction from phenomena to laws and from laws to forces" (ibid., 182).

In his own field of astronomy Laplace believed he had

> explained the laws of the celestial motions, and those of the action of forces producing motion, it remains to compare them together, to determine what forces animate the solar system, and to ascend without the assistance of any hypothesis, but by strict geometrical reasoning, to the principle of universal gravitation, from which they are derived. ([1796] 1830, 2:4:2)

By means of induction and with the aid of mathematical extrapolations, Laplace concluded that the science of astronomy had progressed through three periods. "The first period embraces the observations made by Astronomers antecedently to Copernicus, on the appearances of the celestial motions, and the hypotheses which were devised to explain those appearances, and to subject them to computation." In "the second period, Copernicus deduced from these appearances, the motions of the Earth on its axis and about the Sun, and Kepler discovered the laws of the planetary motions." Finally, "in the third period, Newton, assuming the existence of these laws, established the principle of universal gravitation." Subsequently, "geometers, by applying analysis to this principle, have derived from it all the observed phenomena, and the various inequalities in the motion of the planets, the satellites, and the comets" (ibid., 2:4:324–25).

Thus science is able to discover universal laws (such as gravitation) which can be used to explain the origin of the solar system.

Laplace did not hesitate to call the laws of nature immutable. Indeed, he believed "all the effects of nature are only mathematical results of a small number of immutable laws" ([1814] 1951, 177). For Laplace it was only "in those times of ignorance [that] mankind were far from thinking that nature obeyed immutable laws. . . ." In those days, "whenever any thing happened which seemed out of the natural order, they were considered as so many signs of the anger of heaven [God]" ([1796] 1830, 2:4:48).

One of Laplace's contributions to the development of a modern science of origins was his rejection of what has subsequently been called a God-of-the-gaps mentality. He laments that "formerly, and at no remote epoch, an unusual rain or an extreme drought, a comet having in train a very long tail, the eclipses, the aurora borealis, and in general all the unusual phenomena were regarded as so many signs of celestial wrath. Heaven was invoked in order to avert their baneful influence" ([1814] 1951, 5). However, with the rise of modern scientific observation "no one prayed to have the planets and the sun arrested in their courses: observation had soon made apparent the futility of such prayers" (ibid.). For "all events, even those which on account of their insignificance do not seem to follow the great laws of nature, are a result of it just as necessarily as the revolutions of the sun." It is only "in ignorance of the ties which unite such events to the entire system of the universe, they have been made to depend upon final causes or upon hazard [chance] . . ." (ibid., 3).

Even Isaac Newton had posited the divine intervention of a primary cause (God) to explain what he perceived as an irregular orbit of some planets. This was a violation of the basic nature of operation science. Laplace wrote, "I must here remark how Newton has erred on this point, from the method which he has otherwise so happily applied" ([1796] 1830, 2:4:331). Newton held that a blind force "could never make all the planets move thus, with some irregularities hardly perceivable. . . ." But Laplace responded:

> Could not this arrangement of the planets be itself an effect of the laws of motion; and could not the supreme intelligence which Newton makes to interfere, make it to depend on a more general phenomenon? such as, according to us, a nebulous matter distributed in various masses throughout the immensity of the heavens. Can one even affirm that the preservation of the planetary system entered into the views of the Author of Nature? (Ibid., 2:4:332)

According to Laplace, the kind of error Newton made arises when "the imagination, impatient to arrive at the causes, takes pleasure in creating hypotheses, and often it changes the facts in order to adapt them to its work" (Laplace [1814] 1951, 183). On the contrary, Laplace believed that when one regards only "the means of connecting the phenomena in order to discover the laws; when, by refusing to attribute them to a reality, one rectifies them continually by new observations, they are able to lead to the veritable causes, or at least put us in a position to conclude from the phenomena observed those which given circumstances ought to produce" (ibid., 18).

For Laplace, science is a slow and laborious task. But patience will pay off in the discovery of natural causes. A scientist should not invoke divine intervention to cover up human ignorance.

The true method of science is based on observed regularities, not on singularities. According to Laplace, Newton violated his own discovery of a universal principle of gravitation when he posited the intervention of God to account for certain perceived irregularities. Science is not grounded in the irregular. An unlimited number of causes can be attributed to an event, so "it is necessary, in place of the probability of the event resulting from each cause, to employ the product of this probability by the possibility of the cause itself" (ibid.).

Laplace laid down the principle that "each of the causes to which an observed event may be attributed is indicated with just as much likelihood as there is probability that the event will take place, supposing the event to be constant." Hence, "this principle gives the reason why we attribute regular events to a particular cause" (ibid, 16). In brief, "we are again forced to recognize here the effect of a regular cause" (ibid., 98). That is, we must posit the same kind of cause for an event with which it appears regularly. Hence, "it follows again from this theorem that in a series of events indefinitely prolonged the action of regular and constant causes ought to prevail in the long run over that of irregular causes" (ibid., 62).

Since we can observe regular causal conjunctions in the present, we can assume like conjunctions held in the past. This is the basis of the principle of uniformity which plays a crucial role in any scientific understanding of the past. The observed present is the key to the unobserved past.

Laplace made use of the principle of uniformity (analogy) in his astronomy, saying, "These arguments are likewise confirmed by analogy." For an east-west rotation, similar to that which the diurnal motion of the heavens seems to indicate in the earth, had been observed in almost all the planets (Laplace [1796] 1830, 1:2:162). Laplace considered it "of the greatest importance to the progress of astronomy" to ascertain what really obtains in nature. He added, "We therefore proceed, under the guidance of induction and analogy, to determine, by a comparison of phenomena, the real motions which produce them, and thence to ascend to the laws of these motions" (ibid., 1:2:159).

Laplace believed "we ought then to regard the present state of the universe as the effect of its anterior state and as the cause of the one which is to follow" ([1814] 1951, 4). So "present events are connected with preceding ones by a tie based upon the evident principle that a thing cannot occur without a cause which produces it." Laplace contended that the principle of causality "extends even to actions which are considered indifferent." For even "the freest will is unable without a determinative motive to give them birth" (ibid., 3). Otherwise we would have to assume the absurdity of "an effect without a cause" (ibid., 4). Thus the universe is an unbroken, continuous series of physical causes.

Every event has a cause, but the only way we can know scientifically which causes produced which effects is by observing the regularity of occurrences and analyzing probabilities. For we are able "by the analysis of probabilities, to verify the existence or the influence of certain causes whose action is believed to exist upon organized beings" (ibid., 104). Thus "analogy is based upon the probability that similar things have causes of the same kind and produce the same effects" and "this probability increases as the similitude becomes more perfect" (ibid., 180).

In some cases the probability of casual connection is so high as to make it virtually certain. However, "the calculus of probabilities . . . appreciates the greatest improbability of testimonies in regard to extraordinary facts" (ibid., 114). And "there are things so extraordinary that nothing can balance their improbability" (ibid., 119). Such are the claims for miracles. Hence,

> one may judge by this the immense weight of testimonies necessary to admit a suspension of natural laws, and how improper it would be to apply to this case the ordinary rules of criticism. All those who without offering this immensity of testimonies support this when making recitals of events contrary to those laws, decrease rather than augment the belief which they wish to inspire; for then those recitals render very probable the error or the falsehood of their authors. (Ibid., 118)

Laplace then developed his own purely naturalistic explanation of the origin of the universe—the nebular hypothesis.

> In the primitive state where we imagine the sun it resembled the nebulae that the telescope shows us composed of a nucleus more or less brilliant surrounded by a nebula which, condensing at the surface, ought to transform it some day into a star. If one conceives by analogy

all the stars formed in this manner, one can imagine their anterior state of nebulosity itself preceded by other stars in which the nebulous matter was more and more diffuse, the nucleus being less and less luminous and dense. Going back, then, as far as possible, one would arrive at a nebulosity so diffuse that one would be able scarcely to suspect its existence. (Ibid., 99)

Laplace saw clearly that his scientific speculations were derived with "the aid of proofs drawn from these analogies [with the present]" (ibid., 100). But this is how he believed a science of origins works. It is based on the principle of uniformity (or analogy), which says that the kind of cause regularly observed to produce a certain kind of effect in the present was probably the same kind of cause that produced it in the past.

Summary and Conclusion

In contrast to ancient and medieval cosmogonies, early scientific views in astronomy were based on observation of natural processes. The earliest modern astronomers derived their belief from a theistic conviction that there is a primary cause (God) who operates his universe in an orderly and regular way. Nevertheless, by stressing the regularity of nature and the need to observe and experiment, they succeeded in discovering widely applicable natural laws (secondary causes) which do not require supernatural intervention into the regular operation of the universe. In fact, the universe came to be viewed by many as a continuous, unbroken series of physical causes. Thus modern science of origins, with its emphasis on secondary causes, came to reject the need for positing any supernatural (primary) cause of events in the natural universe.

However, by eliminating the need for a primary cause altogether, modern science goes too far. Indeed, Laplace made the opposite mistake of Newton. Newton violated the principles of operation science by citing supernatural intervention to explain the regular operation of planets in elliptical orbits. Laplace tended toward the opposite extreme, which would rule out the feasibility of any supernatural cause of the various singular events of origins. Both extremes have proven harmful for science. Newton's mistake would, if applied widely, undermine the realm of operation science. And the other error would largely eliminate the area of origin science, except perhaps for the origin of matter. However, with the rise of the big bang theory, which deals with a discontinuous singularity, the universe is no longer be viewed as an eternal, continuous, unbroken series of physical causes (see chaps. 5–6). Thus the door for a supernatural view is not closed, as Laplace thought.

4

The Emergence of a Naturalistic Approach to Origins in Geology and Biology

Spurred on by the success in astronomy, men like James Hutton and Charles Lyell eventually sought similar natural laws to explain the geological formations of earth. Hence, the principles of uniformity and secondary causality moved to the forefront of scientific views about origins. The result eventually was that scientists postulated that the origin of the earth came about through uniformitarianism rather than catastrophism. There remained, however, one major area for which there was no natural explanation of origins—biology. However, with the successes in astronomy and geology in hand, it was believed to be only a matter of time before biology too would yield to a naturalistic explanation.

The discovery of natural (secondary) causes of the origin of living things, as Immanuel Kant had predicted, did not come quickly. In fact, the first efforts were born prematurely. The early attempts to give a naturalistic (evolutionary) explanation of the origin of living things were crude and were not scientifically credible. But eventually, building on the success of Hutton and Lyell in geology, Charles Darwin overcame these obstacles. Thus a biological science of origins took its place alongside naturalistic views given earlier in astronomy and geology.

Early Scientific Views on Geology

James Hutton (1726–1797)

The principles for a scientific study of origins developed by early astronomers were later applied by geologists and biologists. In this area the Scottish geologist James Hutton was a pioneer. His efforts were followed by Lyell in geology and Darwin in biology.

Hutton was an acquaintance of David Hume, who had argued persuasively against allowing any supernatural intrusion into one's scientific understanding of the world. Hume noted that laws of nature are based on uniform observation of repeated instances. But for Hume a miracle is a violation of a law of nature. He concluded that since "a uniform experience amounts to a proof, there is here a direct and full *proof*, from the nature of the fact, against the existence of any miracle" (Hume [1748] 1955, 10.1.123).

Hutton never denied the existence of a supernatural designer of the universe but, like Hume, he strongly opposed interjecting the miraculous into the study of the operation of the universe. Most of his efforts in this regard were directed toward the prevailing belief that geological data were to be explained by a supernatural catastrophe in the Noahican flood. He strove to show rather that "there is no occasion for having recourse to any unnatural supposition of evil, to any destructive accident in nature, or to the agency of any preternatural cause, in explaining that which actually appears" (Hutton 1795, 1:165–66).

Simply because some events in nature are abrupt does not mean that they have a supernatural cause. For example, "a volcano is not made on purpose to frighten superstitious people into fits of piety and devotion, nor to overwhelm devoted cities with destruction" (ibid., 1:146).

In view of the uniform operations of nature Hutton insisted that

> not only are no powers to be employed that are not natural to the globe, no action to be admitted of except those of which we know the principle, and no extraordinary events to be alleged in order to explain a common appearance, the powers of nature are not to be employed in order to destroy the very object of those powers; we are not to make nature act in violation to that order which we actually observe, and in subversion of that end which is to be perceived in the system of created things. (Ibid., 2:547)

For Hutton a naturalistic approach to the world included a belief in the continuity of natural processes. By continuity he meant an unbroken chain of physical causes extending back into the indefinite past. Building a direct parallel between the regularity of astronomical movements and geological processes, Hutton posited a continuous and endless process of nature:

> For having in the natural history of this earth, seen a succession of worlds, we may from this conclude that there is a system in nature; in like manner as, from seeing revolutions of the planets, it is concluded, that there is a system by which they are intended to continue those revolutions. (Ibid., 1:200)

However, "if the succession of worlds is established in the system of nature, it is in vain to look for any thing higher in the origin of the earth." The "result, therefore, of this physical inquiry is, that we find no vestige of a beginning,—no prospect of an end" (ibid., 1:200).

Thus the operational laws of nature are permanent (ibid., 2:378–79). Each event has an antecedent cause with which it is continuous, and so on without beginning or end. Hutton rejected the criticism that this view demanded an atheistic conclusion that there was no eternal Creator, saying, "Are we thus to measure eternity, that boundless thought, with those physical notions of ours which necessarily limit both space and time? and, because we see not the beginning of created things, Are we to conclude that those things which we see have always been, or been without a cause?" (ibid., 1:222).

Indeed, Hutton might have added that no less than the noted Christian thinker Thomas Aquinas allowed the philosophical possibility (which he rejected on the basis of faith) that the physical universe could be eternal, even though he insisted there would still be a need for a creator creating it from eternity (*Summa theologica* 1.2.3; 1.16.2). In any event, creator or no creator, Hutton insisted that the continuity of nature was an unbroken and endless process.

Another principle which became an essential part of the modern scientific approach to origins is the principle of uniformity. Since the past is not known directly, "we are under a necessity, therefore, of making regular suppositions, in order to come at certain conclusions which may be compared with the present state of things" (Hutton 1795, 1:196). Without such an assumption that the past was like the present there would be no way to know the past. Thus the present is the key to the past. That is, the universe operated in the past in the same basic way it operates in the present, or at least it is reasonable to think so.

Furthermore, the principle of uniformity enables us to make scientific generalizations and explanations. But

when philosophers propose vague theories of the earth, theories
which contain no principle for investigating either the general disorder
of strata or the particular form of mountains, such theories can receive
no confirmation from the examination of the earth, nor can they afford
any rule by which the phenomena in question might be explained.
(Ibid., 2:404)

Without such a uniformitarian understanding of origins, a truly
scientific approach to the past is impossible. But with this principle
of uniformity, even though we cannot immediately observe those
changes of physical objects, "we have, in science, the means of reasoning from distant events; consequently, of discovering, in the general powers of nature, causes for those events of which we see the
effects" (ibid., 1:30–31).

Like Hume ([1748] 1955, 10.1.118), Hutton believed that a scientific argument based on uniformity is tantamount to a proof or demonstration. He believed that whatever conclusions are derived by
means of this science "must be held as evidence, where more immediate proof cannot be obtained." And "in a physical subject, where
things actual are concerned, and not the imaginations of the human
mind, this proof will be considered as amounting to a demonstration"
(Hutton 1795, 1:32).

So by means of uniformity one can approach the past with a
reasonable measure of scientific certainty. Of course, the belief in
"certainty" diminished considerably as the century passed, even
though the belief in uniformity did not.

Charles Lyell (1797–1875)

Where Hutton left off, Lyell began. Like most early scientists, he
saw no contradiction between his belief in uniform natural laws and
the existence of an intelligent designer of the world. In fact, Lyell
believed that God created these laws. He wrote,

In the planetary motions, where geometry has carried the eye so far,
both into the future and the past, we discover no mark either of the
commencement or termination of the present order. It is unreason-
able, indeed, to suppose that such marks should anywhere exist. The
Author of Nature has not given laws to the universe, which, like the
institutions of men, carry in themselves the elements of their own
destruction. ([1830–33] 1887, 78)

This being the case, whether or not one believes in a creator is irrelevant to a truly scientific approach to origins. For Lyell what is necessary is that a scientist follows certain basic principles when studying the world.

Following Hutton, Lyell held that the most important scientific principle in studying the past is the principle of uniformity. By uniformity in nature he meant that the same forces are at work today that were operating in the past. This he clearly stated on the title page of his book: "Principles of Geology, Being an Attempt to Explain the Former Changes of the Earth's Surface, *by Reference to Causes Now in Operation*" (emphasis added). For a scientist it means that "his reliance need not be shaken in the unvarying constancy of the laws of nature, or in his power of reasoning from the present to the past in regard to the changes of the terrestrial system, whether in the organic or inorganic world, . . ." (ibid., 171). Thus those who firmly believe in the uniformity of present and past have "a key to the interpretation of some mysteries in the past" (ibid., 319).

Lyell rejected the discontinuity between living things proposed by Sir Humphry Davy, because Lyell saw a natural continuity in the progression from lower to higher animals found in the fossil record (ibid., 143). But despite his insistence on a general uniformity of past and present, Lyell was alert to avoid the opposite extreme. He denied that the order of nature has, "from the earliest periods, been uniform in the same sense in which we believe it to be uniform at present, and expect it to remain so in future" (ibid., 167).

In general, uniformity means to argue from what is known in the present to the unknown in the past by means of analogy. It is to reason "consistently with the analogy of what is known both of the past and present economy of our system" (ibid., 299).

In spite of his apparent limitation of uniformity to past and present physical force (i.e., secondary causes), Lyell did apply the principle of uniformity to archaeology, which involves a primary cause. He wrote,

> The canoes and stone hatchets, called celts, found in our peat-bogs and estuary deposits, afford an insight into the rude arts and manners of a prehistoric race, to whom the use of metals was unknown, while flint implements of a much ruder type point to a still earlier period, when man coexisted in Europe with many quadrupeds long since extinct. (Ibid., 3–4)

However, without some observational knowledge in the present that these kinds of artifacts had certain kinds of causes, there would be no way of explaining the origin of similar ones in the past. Uniformity (analogy) is the key to knowledge of the past, both historical and scientific.

Like Hutton, Lyell believed in the continuity of present and past, albeit Lyell did not see it as necessarily a beginningless (or endless) continuity. Unlike Hutton, Lyell was not opposed to positing a beginning or end to the physical universe. For the Creator "has not permitted in His works any symptom of infancy or of old age, or any sign by which we may estimate either their future or their past duration. He *may put an end, as He no doubt gave a beginning*, to the present system, at some determinate period of time" (emphasis added). But despite this beginning the principles of continuity and uniformity remain firm. For "we may rest assured that this great catastrophe [of creation] will not be brought about by the laws now existing, and that it is not indicated by anything which we perceive" (ibid., 78). Hence, Lyell admitted in principle the basic tenets of origin science, an analogy to primary causes known in the present and applied to the origin of the universe. Lyell also saw that the act of creating this past singularity of origin is unlike any of the laws by which the universe operates in the present. However, once creation occurred all things continue as from the beginning in a natural way, even though the creation itself would be a supernatural act. Indeed, Lyell pointed out that

> the same men who, as natural philosophers, would have been most incredulous respecting any extraordinary deviations from the known course of nature, if reported to have happened *in their own time*, were equally disposed, as geologists, to expect the proofs of such deviations at every period of the past. (Ibid., 101–2, emphasis added)

Lyell did, however, insist that if a modern scientist firmly believes in the resemblance of the ancient and present system of geological changes, "he will regard every fact collected respecting the causes in diurnal action as affording him a key to the interpretation of some mystery in the past" (ibid., 319). That is to say, belief in continuity of past and present affords scientists a way of understanding what may be otherwise inexplicable events of the past.

Lyell did not accept the concept of biological evolution until the tenth printing of his *Principles of Geology* (1868). However, he eventually admitted this one exception of evolution to the overall observed uniformity of past and present. For he came to believe that one's reliance need not be shaken in the unvarying constancy of the laws of nature, or in his power of reasoning from the present to the past in regard to the changes of the terrestrial system, whether in the organic or inorganic world, provided that he does not deny, in the organic world at least, the possibility of a law of evolution and progress. (Ibid., 171)

But Lyell conceded this only after Darwin had offered evidence that there was a connection between observed changes in the present and evolutionary changes in the past. The principle of uniformity must apply in biology as well as in geology and astronomy.

For Lyell the principles of continuity and uniformity demand a naturalistic approach to both land and life. For

by degrees, many of the enigmas of the moral and physical world are explained, and, instead of being due to extrinsic and irregular causes, they are found to depend on fixed and invariable laws. The philosopher at last becomes convinced of the undeviating uniformity of secondary causes; and, guided by his faith in this principle, he determines the probability of accounts transmitted to him of former occurrences, and often rejects the fabulous tales of former times, on the ground of their being irreconcilable with the experience of more enlightened ages. (Ibid., 89)

In this way it became necessary to reject former explanations which "refer the phenomenon to the command of the Deity . . ." (ibid., 60). The intervention of a creator should not be posited to fill in supposed gaps in the operation of the natural world. For Lyell the progress in natural explanations, coupled with the principle of uniformity, gives ample assurance that there are natural explanations yet to be found for the thus far unexplained anomalies of the functioning of the natural world.

Francis Bacon had implied a distinction between primary and secondary causes ([1620] 1960, 2:2:1) of which Hutton and especially Lyell made fuller use. Many scientists of the seventeenth and eighteenth centuries allowed a creator or first cause of the universe. They believed this creator to be the primary cause of the universe, but the natural laws instituted by the Creator were in the realm of secondary causes. Although Galileo had a similar emphasis, it is credited to Hutton and Lyell that modern geology has subsequently limited itself to the study of these secondary (natural) causes. Speculations about the existence of a primary cause (creator) of origins are left largely for other disciplines. Lyell said that Hutton's treatise on geology (1795) "was the first in which geology was declared to be in no way concerned about 'questions as to the origin of things;' the first in which an attempt was made to dispense entirely with all hypothetical causes, and to explain the former changes of the earth's crust by reference exclusively to natural agents" (Lyell [1830–33] 1887, 73).

This is an important turning point in the development of the modern scientific approach to origins. While some theists claimed that limiting science to the study of secondary (natural) causes was atheistic, others insisted that it glorified the perfection of the Creator that he established such perfect regularity in his creation (ibid., 80, 91). Still others did not believe in the need for a first cause but simply accepted a beginningless process of natural events. Their view was purely naturalistic (see appendix 2).

Regardless of their beliefs about God, scientists came to accept the methodological limitation of this distinction between primary and secondary causes. And from the time of Lyell onward geologists looked increasingly for only natural (secondary) causes of earth's phenomena, leaving behind the supernatural (theistic) cosmogonies of earlier writers for a more strictly naturalistic approach. In Lyell's words,

> The most common and serious source of confusion arose from the notion, that it was the business of geology to discover the mode in which the earth originated, or, as some imagined, to study the effects of those cosmological causes which were employed by the Author of Nature to bring this planet out of a nascent and chaotic state into a more perfect and habitable condition. (Ibid., 4)

A rare phenomenon scarcely ever fails to excite a suspicion of the supernatural "in those minds which are not firmly convinced of the uniform agency of secondary causes," Lyell observed (ibid., 94). However, he believed that when secondary causes were wedded to the principle of uniformity it becomes entirely unnecessary to posit anything but natural causes for past events in the universe.

For Lyell the essential difference between a scientific and an unscientific approach to the past is that science is based on observations of a regular pattern of events, whereas nonscientific views are based on speculations. Since the universe operates by uniform natural laws on which science is built, he believed that the only hope for a scientific understanding of the origin of the world and life is one based on observations in the present.

According to Lyell, whenever he is challenged the scientist is satisfied with the advice to "go and see" (ibid., 72). Only those who could find no basis in present observation resort to positing supernatural causes for events. But once science limits itself to observation of the regular process of nature it is automatically limited to secondary causes. Thus Lyell did for geology what Georges Louis Leclerc de Buffon and Pierre Simon de Laplace did for astronomy—established it as a natural science in pursuit only of secondary causes.

Early Naturalistic Views on Biology

Pre-Darwinian Biology

The theory of evolution has roots in antiquity. The Greeks and Hindus had naturalistic views of origins. Like modern evolutionists, neither made appeal to supernatural causes beyond the universe (as many theists do).

Although Greeks did not think of evolution in the Darwinian, gradualistic, progressive sense, they did have naturalistic theories of origin in which animals and man emerged from lower forms of life. One Greek explanation of origins centered around the principles of love (attraction) and strife (repulsion):

> First sprang up from the earth whole-natured forms, having a share of both water and fire; these the fire sent forth, desiring to reach its like, showing forth as yet neither the lovely form of the limbs, nor the voice nor the organ proper to men.

> There is a further question, too, which might be asked. Is it possible or impossible that bodies in unordered movement should combine in some cases into combinations like those of which bodies of nature's composing are composed, such, I mean, as bones and flesh? Yet this is what Empedocles [a fifth-century philosopher] asserts to have occurred under Love. 'Many a head', says he, 'came to birth without a neck.' . . . as Empedocles said that 'where heads of many creatures came to birth without necks', they are then put together by Love. . . .

> At the same time he asserts that the world is in the same state now in the period of Strife as it was earlier in that of Love. [Kirk and Raven 1957, 241]

According to John Burnet, "Empedocles was guided by the idea of the survival of the fittest" ([1892] 1967, 243). Aristotle rejected Empedocles' view because it left too much to chance (Aristotle *Physics* B, 8.198629, RP 173a). It is clear, however, that Greek science did not have an empirical basis (see chap. 2). Hence, for centuries no real progress was made in a naturalistic understanding of human origins. Nonetheless, naturalistic views of origin, along with other Greek ideas, had a renaissance in the sixteenth and seventeenth centuries.

Most Greek views about evolution were based largely on philosophical speculation and lacked a solid empirical (observational) footing. The evolutionary views of Auguste Comte (1798–1857) also fit into this category. Even the evolutionary conclusions of Herbert Spencer (1820–1903) were largely philosophical (speculative) in nature. The first faltering attempts to give evolution a scientific basis were made by Jean Baptiste Lamarck (1744–1829) and Robert Chambers (1802–1871).

Lamarck was strongly influenced by Buffon and had actually worked with him. Using the success in astronomy (of Laplace and Buffon) as a model, Lamarck asked: Granting that the earth began as a formless mass, by what evolutionary process did the present biological world emerge out of lifeless matter?

Lamarck's contribution to the evolutionary debate was primarily geological. He pointed to a clear organic progression in the fossil record. The older the rocks, the simpler were the life forms they contained (Toulmin and Goodfield 1967, 219).

However, Lamarck is primarily remembered for his failure. He posited the inheritance of acquired characteristics as a modus operandi of evolution, declaring boldly, "*Species* have only a limited or temporary constancy in their characters, and . . . there is no species which is absolutely constant. Doubtless they will subsist unchanged in the places in which they inhabit so long as the circumstances which affect them do not change, and do not force them to change their habits of life" (cited in ibid.). Sometimes the development of new limbs or organs was, Lamarck believed, the unconscious response of animals adjusting to new conditions in their environment.

Since Lamarck, unlike most of his contemporaries, started with a prejudice in favor of evolution, the burden of proof was on him. And since there was a great gap between the theory of inheriting acquired characteristics and the actual scientific evidence, Lamarckianism lost the day.

One of the most controversial pre-Darwinian attempts to establish evolution was made by Robert Chambers in *Vestiges of the Natural History of Creation* (1844). Chambers was firmly convinced that the physical laws recently applied with great success in astronomy and geology were equally applicable to biology. Three scientific principles stood out: uniformity, continuity, and natural (secondary) causality. Chambers wrote:

> If there is anything more than another impressed on our minds by the course of the geological history, it is, that the same laws and conditions of nature now apparent to us have existed throughout the whole time, though the operation of some of these laws may now be less conspicuous than in the early ages, from some of the conditions having come to a settlement and a close. ([1844] 1969, 146)

In view of the religious climate of his day Chambers was careful not to exclude God. However, God was limited to a deistic role of creating natural laws by which everything unfolded. Chambers believed that

> the progress of organic life upon our earth, is that the simplest and most primitive type, under a law to which that of like-production is subordinate, gave birth to the type next above it, that this again produced the next higher, and so on to the very highest, the stages of advance being in all cases very small—namely, from one species only to another; so that the phenomenon has always been of a simple and modest character. (Ibid., 222)

Chambers dismissed Lamarck summarily in view of what he believed to be superior light from geology and physiology. However, he offered no real mechanism for evolution and made unfounded claims such as spontaneous generation of clover from lime-covered ground, the transmutation of rye from cropped oats, and a fish developing a reptile heart. In Chambers's words,

> It is no great boldness to surmise that a super-adequacy in the measure of this under-adequacy (and the one thing seems as natural an occurrence as the other) would suffice in a goose to give its progeny the body of a rat, and produce the ornithorhynchus, or might give the progeny of an ornithorhynchus the mouth and feet of a true rodent, and thus complete at two stages the passage from the aves to the mammalia. (Ibid., 221)

The lack of a credible scientific explanation for Chambers's views earned him the scorn of even other evolutionists. T. H. Huxley reacted violently, calling it a work produced by a "prodigious ignorance and thoroughly unscientific habit of mind" (cited by Gillispie [1951] 1959, 163). Darwin was milder in the introduction to the first edition of *Origin of Species* but he still wrote contemptuously, "The author of the 'Vestiges of Creation' would I presume say, that after a certain number of unknown generations, some bird had given birth to a woodpecker, and some plant to a misseltoe [sic], and that these had been produced perfect as we now see them" (ibid., 220). Darwin believed Chambers's "geology is bad and his zoology is worse." In Darwin's copy of *Vestiges* he wrote: "the idea of a fish passing into a reptile, monstrous" (cited by Himmelfarb 1962, 220–21).

In summary, like astronomers and geologists of their time, some pre-Darwinian biologists believed in evolution. They too based this belief on certain principles by which they believed the origin of living things should be approached. These beliefs included the following:

1. Uniformity in nature
2. Continuity of nature
3. Secondary (natural) causality

But unlike astronomers and geologists, pre-Darwinian biologists were unable to provide a credible naturalistic explanation for evolution. No observable, testable mechanism or secondary cause for evolution was known.

Charles Darwin (1809–1882)

What Lyell accomplished by applying the newly developed principles of science to historical geology Darwin did for historical biology. Evolutionists before Darwin had failed to offer a credible causal mechanism for the origin of species. Darwin's success was built on Lyell's foundation. He admitted the influence of Lyell as early as his voyage on the *Beagle* (Darwin 1888, 1:263). A decade later he dedicated the revised edition of the *Journal* to Lyell, admitting, "I always feel as if my books came half out of Lyell's brain . . ." (Aug. 29, 1844; ibid., 2:117).

Darwin accepted the theory of evolution before he had scientific support for it. Indeed, George Grinnell recently reiterated this point:

"I have done a great deal of work on Darwin and can say with some assurance that Darwin also did not derive his theory from nature but rather superimposed a certain philosophical world-view on nature and then spent 20 years trying to gather the facts to make it stick" (1972, 44).

It is credited to Darwin (and Alfred Wallace) that a purely natural principle (natural selection) observable in the present was applied to the origin of species. Darwin succeeded in overthrowing the dominance of what he called "the theory of creation" ([1859] 1958, 435, 437) with his newly developed mechanism for evolution. It is clear that he was able to do this by borrowing the kind of naturalistic principles (uniformity and secondary causes) of modern science already operative in astronomy and geology and then applying them to biology. Darwin acknowledged this connection by noting that the widespread unwillingness in his day to acknowledge the common ancestry of species "is the same as that felt by so many geologists, when Lyell first insisted that long lines of inland cliffs had been formed, the great valleys excavated, by the agencies which we see still at work" (ibid., 443).

It is evident that Darwin limited his scientific study of origins to secondary causes. He did acknowledge in his second edition of *The Origin of Species* (printed thereafter) that the very first form(s) of life may have been created by a primary cause (creator). In the last lines of this and following editions of *Origin* Darwin said, "There is grandeur in this view of life, with its several powers, having been originally breathed by the Creator into a few forms or into one" (ibid., 450). However, eventually Darwin was skeptical about the need for a primary cause of the first form of life, declaring "that the whole subject is beyond the scope of man's intellect. . . . The mystery of the beginning of all things is insoluble by us; and I for one must be content to remain an Agnostic" (cited by Edwards 1967, 4:295). Darwin even privately speculated in a letter (1870) about a "warm little pond" in which first life may have arisen by purely natural means.

Despite his uncertainty about the need for an initial creator of life Darwin was sure about the need for natural causes of biological origins of species. He wrote, "It accords with what we know of the law impressed on matter by the Creator, that the creation and extinction of forms, like the birth and death of individuals should be the effect of secondary . . . means" (Moore 1979, 326). As early as 1844 Darwin wrote, ". . . let us consider whether there exists any secondary means in the economy of nature by which the process of selection could go on adapting, nicely and wonderfully, organisms . . . to diverse ends" (ibid., 323). Eventually confident that he had found such a cause in natural selection, Darwin referred to it as "my deity 'Natural Selection'" (ibid., 322). In other words he believed he had discovered a natural cause for the origin of species which had replaced the need to appeal to a supernatural primary cause (the Deity).

Darwin believed it was beneath the dignity of a creator to create each species directly and separately. Even earlier, when he believed in a creator, Darwin wrote, "I am inclined to look at everything as resulting from designed laws, with the details, whether good or bad, left to the working out of what we may call chance" (Darwin 1888, 1:279; 2:105). In contrast to the creationists of his day, Darwin declared, "Authors of the highest eminence seem to be fully satisfied with the view that each species has been independently created. To my mind it accords better with what we know of the laws impressed on matter by the Creator" ([1859] 1958, 449).

Darwin opposed stating that a creator made the various kinds of life simply because one is ignorant of a natural cause. For, he warned, "it is so easy to hide our ignorance under such expressions as the 'plan of creation,' 'unity of design,' . . . , and to think that we give an explanation when we only re-state a fact" (ibid., 444). Darwin found it easier to believe there was a void in our understanding of nature than that it "required a fresh act of creation to supply the voids caused by the action of His [the Creator's] laws" (ibid., 443). The principle of economy of causes alone would resist positing multiple acts of creation.

Darwin referred to the creationist explanation of specially created adaptation to environment as "trash" (see Moore 1979, 312). He argued that the theory of special creation is not really a scientific explanation:

> The explanation of types of structure in classes—as resulting from the *will* of the Deity, to create animals on certain plans,—is no explanation—*it has not the character of a physical law &* is therefore utterly useless. —it foretells nothing because we know nothing of the will of the Deity, how it acts & whether constant or inconstant like that of man. (Ibid., 318, emphasis added)

Here it is evident that Darwin is confusing operation science and origin science. Darwin is not willing to admit that anything but an operational law (i.e., a secondary cause) counts as an explanation. Hence, for Darwin natural selection is such a law, but special creation is not. Science deals with how the universe operates, not with why it came to be (cited in ibid.). Species "have all been produced by laws acting around us" (Darwin [1859] 1958, 450). The belief in "abrupt modifications" or creation is not "a scientific point of view." It is not built on any testable operational law of the world from which predictions can be made "leading to further investigations" (ibid., 445). For Darwin, "nature makes no jumps." "Therefore, if we want to know whether something that interests us is of natural origin or supernatural, we must ask: did it arise gradually out of that which came before, or suddenly without any evident natural cause?" (Denton 1986, 58).

So firmly did Darwin believe he had discovered a natural operational law of the universe which could explain the origin of species that he compared the natural processes of evolution to the law of gravity, saying,

> For my part I could no more admit the . . . proposition [that "each of . . . three species of rhinoceros, were separately created with deceptive appearances of true relationship"] than I could admit that the planets move in their courses, and that a stone falls to the ground, not through the intervention of the secondary and appointed law of gravity, but from the direct volition of the Creator. (Moore 1979, 326)

.   The whole case for common ancestry is built on the assumption of a continuity of past and present on which one can base a theory about past origins. Natural selection can be observed in the present and hence should be assumed to have occurred in the past. Evolution means descent with modification, and "Natural Selection has been the most important, but not the exclusive, means of modification" (Matthews 1971, 30).

Darwin was so completely convinced of the continuity of natural causes in the biological realm that he posited an unbroken chain of small changes from all living species to possibly one common ancestor. Darwin was cautious not to overstate his case; he claimed that there may have been a "few" original created forms. However, as some scholars have noted, "a polyphyletic origin of life is incompatible with the principle of phylogenetic continuity" which Darwin embraced (Adler [1967] 1968, 72). Common ancestry logically leads to a singular origin.

Darwin was aware that no such finely graded continuity was represented in the fossil record. However, he speculated that this is because "the geological record is the history of the world imperfectly kept . . ." ([1859] 1958, 312). We have at best only a few lines of a few pages of a few chapters of the whole paleontological record. But Darwin believed the existing fossils were a sufficient sample on which to base the argument that if we had a complete record of past life there would be no gaps. Darwin was convinced that the biological world, like the physical world, is a continuous whole. It has no biological potholes caused by creative interruptions in the grand orderliness of the laws of nature.

Summary and Conclusion

The modern naturalistic theories of origins began by taking the operational laws of physics and applying them to astronomy. Building on this success, geologists applied physical laws to past events to overthrow creationist views in favor of a naturalistic approach to origins. Eventually, Darwin did the same for biology. Thus each major sphere of modern science had established a purely naturalistic approach to the question of origins. Gradually appeal to a supernatural (primary) cause was dropped as a credible scientific approach to origins.

The key principles in this naturalistic approach to origins were uniformity, continuity, and secondary causality. The principle of uniformity declares that the present is the key to the past. This is based in turn on the belief that there is an unbroken chain or continuity of causes extending into the indefinite past. Of course the principle of continuity suffered a severe blow with the advent of the big bang theory of origin, which entails a radical discontinuity in physical causation.

It was not important to naturalistic scientists whether or not there was a first (primary) cause of the universe. What was important to them was limiting science to the study of secondary (natural) causes. By the application of the three principles—uniformity, continuity, and secondary causality—the earlier theistic cosmogonies gave way to purely naturalistic cosmologies. The domain of origin science was taken over by operation science. Even the unique, unrepeated events of the origin of the universe, of life, and of new life forms were treated as though they were observed regularities in the present. The difference between unobserved past singularities (origin science) and observed present regularities (operation science) was obscured. The search for natural (secondary) causes for how the universe and life operate in the present was gradually extended to how they originated in the past. Overlooked was the fact that events of origin are not a recurring pattern of events against which a theory of origin can be tested. Hence, even the very naturalistic theories of origin, which had replaced the supernaturalistic ones, would lack scientific status unless a special category is made for them. Such is possible by distinguishing origin science from operation science (as forensic science differs from empirical science). However, once this difference is recognized, then the possibility of creationism as science is again resurrected, and we have come full circle.

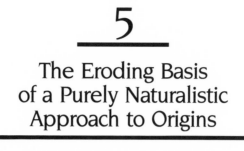

5

The Eroding Basis
of a Purely Naturalistic
Approach to Origins

The Development of a Naturalistic Approach to Origins

A naturalistic approach to origin science began slowly. Gradually the legitimate search for natural (secondary) causes in operation science was applied to origin science. First astronomy, then geology and biology were taken over by a growing naturalism. Eventually even the origin of life itself was explained by purely natural causes (see chap. 7).

The Major Principles of Modern Science

Having traced the major movements leading to a modern naturalistic approach to origins, let us consider the principles on which it rests. They consist of three:

1. The belief in the continuity of present and past.
2. The search for secondary or natural causes of past events.
3. The principle of uniformity, which says the present is the key to the past.

These premises are actually interrelated. For the uniformity between the present and past is related to an assumed continuity in nature and offers a basis for expecting the same kinds of natural cause in the past which we see for similar events in the present. But uniformity is the functional key to the other two principles, since observed regularities in the present enable us to posit secondary causes of past events which thereby are known to stand in continuity to present ones. A scientific understanding of the past is based firmly on the principle of uniformity. But the principle of uniformity appears to be violated by miracles. Thus modern science by its very nature seems to reject the possibility of supernatural intervention into the world.

The chronology of how this naturalistic approach to the past developed has been traced in previous chapters. The principles of mathematics and physics were applied first to astronomy, then to geology, and finally to biology. Beginning with the Greek (Pythagorean) idea of a mathematically analyzable universe, early scientists (such as Galileo) discovered certain physical laws (like acceleration). These physical laws, believed to be created manifestations of God's very thoughts, were applied to the astronomical realm (by Johannes Kepler) with revolutionary success.

Inspired by the success of astronomers in using physical laws to explain the history of the heavens, geologists (James Hutton, Charles Lyell) applied this procedure to the study of the earth. Biologists (particularly Charles Darwin) sought physical causes to explain the origin of species. And eventually this same search for a natural explanation would be applied (by Stanley Miller and Harold C. Urey) to the origin of life itself from nonliving chemicals (see chap. 7).

Now behind this whole science of origins is one fundamental premise on which all science of origins is based, namely, the principle of uniformity. For if the present is not the key to the past, then there is no scientific way to know the past. Since there is no observational evidence of the past events of origins, we are completely dependent on our present observations and on the assumption that there is a uniformity (analogy) between the present and the past. Thus without the principle of uniformity there could be no scientific approach to origins.

The Mistake of Supernaturalists

One of the reasons for the decline of modern creationist views of origins was their ad hoc appeal to the supernatural to explain anomalies in the operation of the universe. Explaining meteors, earthquakes, and other natural irregularities as the results of divine intervention proved to be embarrassing to supernaturalists, for scientists have subsequently found natural explanations for all these events.

Creationists recognized that the Creator (primary cause) works in his creation through natural (secondary) causes. Nonetheless, they sometimes violated this belief by positing a supernatural cause to explain certain anomalies in the operation of the universe. The subsequent discovery of natural (secondary) causes for these events led to an eventual discrediting of an appeal to a supernatural (primary) cause for any event, even the origin of the universe and life.

The very founders of modern science—Bacon, Galileo, Kepler, Newton—were theistically (or deistically) oriented. They laid down the basic approach to the study of the cosmos, namely, the discovery of natural law. They believed a primary cause (creator) set up these natural laws but that operation science deals only with the laws (secondary causes) of nature. Furthermore, these laws are associated with regular, repeating patterns in the observable world. We have good reason to believe these laws remain uniform throughout the ages. However, creationists at times did not clearly distinguish the realm of origin science (e.g., cosmogony) from that of operation science (e.g., cosmology). This eventually led to a rejection by many scientists of any appeal to a primary cause, even in the area of origins.

The Basis of Origin Science in the Principle of Uniformity

From the very beginning of modern science there was a recognition (even by many who believed in a creator) that a scientific approach to the operation of the universe is in terms of secondary (natural) causes. To be sure, this was not always applied consistently by creationists but it was there nonetheless. Noncreationists, however, having no commitment to a creator, assumed that secondary (natural) causes explain the origin and operation of the universe.

At the heart of the objection to invoking the supernatural as a scientific explanation is the principle of uniformity. For if natural causes observed in the present are capable of explaining similar events, why should one assume a supernatural cause for them in the past?

Francis Bacon (1561–1626)

Bacon believed "the beginning is from God." He saw evidence in nature for positing a supernatural cause of origins. For the world, "having the character of good so strongly impressed upon it, appears manifestly to proceed from God, who is the author of good, and the Father of Lights" (Bacon [1620] 1960, 1:93:91–92). However, Bacon was also strongly committed to a naturalistic explanation of the operation of the universe. For the Creator has impressed permanent laws upon his good creation. "In nature nothing really exists besides individual bodies, performing pure individual acts according to a fixed law . . ." (ibid., 2:2:122). Because these laws are there in nature, they can be discovered by experience. "The best demonstration by far is experience, if it go not beyond the actual experiment" (ibid., 1:70:67). The inductive method by which this is accomplished extends not only to natural sciences "but to all sciences" (ibid., 1:127:16).

The sphere in which the scientist was to look for these laws was nature. And by nature Bacon did not mean what the Greeks meant, namely, immutable and eternal forms. For "the investigation of forms, which are . . . eternal and immutable, constitute *Metaphysics.*" But "the investigation of the efficient cause, and of matter and of the latent process . . . constitute *physics*" (ibid., 2:9:129). Nature then consists of temporal, physical forms which can be studied empirically.

So the "true model" or "ideas of the divine" are "the Creator's own stamp upon creation, impressed and defined in matter by true and exquisite lines" (ibid., 1:124:113–14). Hence, the scientist seeks to find the forms (i.e., laws) of the very operations of the natural world (ibid., 2:3:122). Scientific study of the operation of the universe, then, is limited to secondary (natural) causes. For "remote causes [primary causes], without reference to the latent process leading to the form [i.e., law], are but slight and superficial, and contribute little, if anything to true and active science" (ibid., 2:2:121).

Bacon seems to imply in one passage that even alleged miracles, or "prodigies of nature," are to be approached naturalistically. "For in these also we are not to desist from inquiry until the cause of the deviation is discovered" (ibid., 2:29:178). In other words, the supernaturalist does not have the right to place "No Trespass" signs for those studying the operations of the universe.

It is not clear whether Bacon saw the full ramifications of limiting scientific research to secondary (natural) causes. He did speak against those who based their scientific beliefs about nature on a supernatural revelation such as the Bible (ibid., 1:65:62).

Beneath Bacon's rejection of any attempt to found a natural science on the belief in supernatural interventions into natural operations was his belief in the uniformity of the laws of nature. He recognized that without these regular patterns of operation impressed on matter by the Creator there was no true science. Hence, the principle of uniformity is already implied in the view of "the father of modern science."

Thomas Hobbes (1588–1679)

Whatever naturalistic conclusions Bacon may have failed to draw because of his belief in God, Hobbes, with his materialistic perspective, seemed unafraid to declare. Although Hobbes gave lip service to the idea of a creator (perhaps because in his day an outright atheist was in social disfavor), nevertheless his view was fundamentally materialistic:

> The world (I mean not the earth only, that denominates the lovers of it 'worldly men,' but the *universe*, that is, the whole mass of all things that are) is corporeal, that is to say, body; and hath the dimensions of magnitude, namely, length, breadth, and depth: also every part of body is likewise body, and hath the like dimensions; and consequently every part of the universe is body, and that which is not body is no part of the universe: and because the universe is all, that which is no part of it is nothing, and consequently nowhere. Nor does it follow from hence that spirits are nothing: for they have dimensions and are therefore really bodies . . . . (Emphasis added)

As to a so-called incorporeal spirit, such as God, Hobbes insisted that we name God not because we can actually describe his incomprehensible nature, but simply as an expression of our desire to worship him ([1651] 1952, 4:46:269–70).

In accordance with his materialistic beliefs about the world, Hobbes insisted that our knowledge is limited to empirical sensations. "For there is no conception in a man's mind which hath not at first, totally or by parts, been begotten upon the organs of sense" (ibid., 1:1:49). And the cause of sense is the external body. Hence, science does not begin a priori, or independent of experience, with definitions but is

> getting a good and orderly method in proceeding from the elements, which are names, to assertions made by connexion of one of them to another; and so to syllogisms, which are the connexions of one asser-

tion to another, till we come to a knowledge of all the consequences of names appertaining to the subject in hand; and that is it, men call *science*. (Ibid., 1:5:60)

This procedure, of course, is based on sensory observation; "when we see how anything comes about, upon what causes, and by what manner; when the like causes come into our power, we see how to make it produce the like effects" (ibid.).

It is understandable that Hobbes would draw out the naturalistic implications of this principle of uniformity in his view of the world. First of all, he limited the Bible to the realm of faith and allocated all factual knowledge to the domain of science. For "the Scripture was written to show unto men the kingdom of God, and to prepare their minds to become his obedient subjects, leaving the world, and the philosophy thereof, to the disputation of men for the exercising of their natural reason" (ibid., 1:8:70).

Second, Hobbes offered some unprecedented natural explanations where hitherto only supernatural ones had prevailed. The belief in private revelation which men thought they received "supernaturally by |God's| Spirit," Hobbes said, "begins very often from some lucky finding of an error generally held by others" (ibid., 1:8:69). And the alleged demonic cause of "madness" (insanity) Hobbes believed to be nothing but too much passion: "The variety of behaviour in men that have drunk too much is the same with that of madmen" (ibid.). As to any biblical story about demons being cast out, Hobbes believed it to be a "parable." He concluded firmly, "I see nothing at all in the Scripture that requireth a belief that demoniacs were any other thing but madmen" (ibid., 1:8:70–71). The reason men posit supernatural causes for such events is "the want of curiosity to search natural causes" (ibid.). For "they that see any strange and unusual ability or defect in a man's mind, unless they see withal from what cause it may probably proceed, can hardly think it natural; and if not natural, they must needs think it supernatural; and then what can it be, but that either God or the Devil is in him?" (ibid.).

In summation, Hobbes believed that the uniformly observed process of nature would lead us to posit a natural cause, even where we do not know one. For ignorance of a natural cause does not argue for a supernatural one, especially in view of uniform observation that parallel situations can be explained by purely natural causes. The application of this reasoning to origins did not come to fruition for a century or more after Hobbes, but the logical implications of Hobbes's naturalistic views seemed unavoidable.

Benedict Spinoza (1632–1677)

Whatever atheistic implications there may or may not have been in Hobbes's antisupernaturalism in science, there were no such tendencies in Spinoza. He was a clear-cut pantheist. Yet his opposition to the concept of supernatural intervention in the natural world is as strong as any in modern times. Spinoza believed that our mind "partakes of the nature of God, and solely from this cause is enabled to form notions explaining natural phenomena . . ." ([1670] 1951, 14). This is because God has written his laws in our minds. Thus it is evident that all natural phenomena express the conception of God as far as their essence and perfection extend. Thus we have greater and more perfect knowledge of God in proportion to our knowledge of natural phenomena (ibid., 59).

Because God is by nature absolute, necessary, and eternal, and because natural laws are an expression of his nature, these laws too are immutable. As Spinoza put it, "As nothing is necessarily true save only by Divine decree, it is plain that the universal laws of nature are decrees of God following from the necessity and perfection of the Divine nature" (ibid., 83). These laws are necessary and immutable, for "whatever comes to pass, comes to pass according to laws and rules which involve eternal necessity and truth; nature, therefore, always observes laws and rules which involve eternal necessity and truth, although they may not all be known to us, and therefore she keeps a fixed and immutable order" (ibid.). Natural laws embrace everything conceived by the divine intellect. They extend over infinity and work in accordance with "a fixed and immutable order" (ibid., 84–86).

Natural laws are fixed, eternal, and immutable. "Nothing, then, comes to pass in nature in contravention to her universal laws . . ." (ibid., 83). Of course, for Spinoza "nature" is not limited to "matter and its modifications, but infinite other things besides matter" (ibid., 83, n. 1). Nature, however, does include the physical universe. In fact, Spinoza referred to Newton's law of gravity as one such law of nature (ibid., 57).

According to Spinoza, even "Scripture makes the general assertion in several passages that nature's course is fixed and unchangeable" (ibid., 96, referring to Ps. 148:6; Jer. 31:35). He adds that Ecclesiastes 3:11 says, "I know that whatsoever God doeth, it shall be for ever; nothing can be put to it, nor anything taken from it." Spinoza's conclusion from this premise is unequivocal:

> Now, as nothing is necessarily true save only by Divine decree, it is plain that the universal laws of nature are decrees of God following from the necessity and perfection of the Divine nature. Hence, any event happening in nature which contravened nature's universal laws, would necessarily also contravene the Divine decree, nature, and understanding; or if anyone asserted that God acts in contravention to the laws of nature, he, *ipso facto*, would be compelled to assert that God acted against His own nature—an evident absurdity. (Ibid., 83)

Miracles, including creation by a supernatural cause, are impossible, for "miracles, in the sense of events contrary to the laws of nature, so far from demonstrating to us the existence of God, would, on the contrary, lead us to doubt it. . . .""Nature follows a fixed and immutable order" (ibid., 85), and an eternal immutable order cannot be temporarily interrupted. Hence, "when Scripture describes an event as accomplished by God or God's will, we must understand merely that it was in accordance with the law and order of nature. . . ." We cannot believe as most people do "that nature had for a season ceased to act, or that her order was temporarily interrupted" (ibid., 89).

Why, then, do people believe in miracles? Spinoza replies, "Plainly, they are but triflers who, when they cannot explain a thing, run back to the will of God; this is, truly, a ridiculous way of expressing ignorance" (ibid., 86). For "the masses then style unusual phenomena 'miracles,' and partly from piety, partly for the sake of opposing the students of science, prefer to remain in ignorance of natural causes, and only to hear of those things which they know least, and consequently admire most" (ibid., 81).

For Spinoza the rejection of supernatural intervention in nature is not the rejection of God. For nature is God, and God is nature. Indeed, our very knowledge of God's "will increases in proportion to our knowledge and clear understanding of nature, as we see how she depends on her primal [primary] cause, and how she works according to eternal law" (ibid., 86). That is, God works in nature through secondary causes. Hence, "so far as our understanding goes, those phenomena which we clearly and distinctly understand have much better right to be called works of God, and to be referred to the will of God than those about which we are entirely ignorant, although they appeal powerfully to the imagination, and compel men's admiration" (ibid.).

But the "Scripture does not explain things by their secondary causes, but only narrates them . . . to move men, and especially uneducated men, to devotion" (ibid., 91). Therefore, "the Bible leaves reason absolutely free, . . ." and has nothing in common with philosophy and science (ibid., 9). Thus, Spinoza concludes, "it is plain that all the events narrated in Scripture came to pass naturally, and are referred directly to God because Scripture, as we have shown, does not aim at explaining things by their natural causes, but only at narrating what appeals to the popular imagination" (ibid., 90).

Even if "events are found in the Bible which we cannot refer to their causes, nay, which seem entirely to contradict the order of nature, we must not come to a stand, but assuredly believe that whatever did really happen happened naturally" (ibid., 90). To do otherwise would be to suppose wrongly "that God is inactive so long as nature works in her accustomed order, and *vice versa*, that the power of nature and natural causes are idle so long as God is acting" (ibid., 81). For Spinoza this is an unacceptable deistic view of God in which people "imagine the power of God to be like that of some royal potentate, and nature's power to consist in force and energy" (ibid., 81). God is not different from nature; he is one in substance with it ([1677] 1953, 1:5:14, 43, 52).

In summary, there is a distinct difference between the incipient deism of Bacon, the implied atheism of Hobbes, and the explicit pantheism of Spinoza. For a deist, unlike a theist, God created the world but it runs by natural law without divine interruption. For a pantheist there is no absolute distinction between God and the world. But these differences notwithstanding, all agree that science deals with a uniformly regulated nature which reflects the mind of God. They all reject the notion that our study of the natural world should consider divine interruptions. Uniformity of nature present and past is the key to understanding her operations. And philosophical or religious beliefs of the scientists notwithstanding, all three of these men believed that scientists as scientists should approach the operations of the world in a naturalistic way, looking only for secondary causes.

David Hume (1711–1776)

Almost a century went by before Hume laid down his argument for uniformity in the study of nature. Because of his empirical, a posteriori approach to the world (in the tradition of Bacon), Hume saw clearly what others with more a priori, rationalistic approaches had missed. Hume agreed with Bacon, who viewed science as the seeking of the appropriate natural causes for the observed effects. And Hume saw that all reasoning from effect to cause is based on custom or habit. That is,

> a customary conjunction between that and some other object; or, in other words, having found, in many instances, that any two kinds of objects, flame and heat, snow and cold, have always been conjoined together: if flame or snow be presented anew to the senses, the mind is carried by custom to expect heat or cold, and to *believe* that such a quality does exist and will discover itself upon a nearer approach. ([1748] 1955, 5:1:60, emphasis added)

So "custom, then, is the great guide of human life. It is that principle alone which renders our experience useful to us and makes us expect, for the future, a similar train of events with those which have appeared in the past" (ibid., 5:1:58). In fact, without customary observed conjunctions we would "be entirely ignorant of every matter of fact beyond what is immediately present to the memory and senses" (ibid., 5:1:58–59). Thus only uniformly observed conjunctions in the present enable us to speak of the past or of the future. It was Hume's acquaintance, James Hutton, who was credited with applying this naturalistic view of the history of the earth and concluding that the same natural causes we regularly observe in the present were at work in the past as well.

Hume saw a great utility in our understanding of the past (or future) being based on customarily observed conjunctions of events. He saw it as "a kind of pre-established harmony" between nature and our minds. He spoke of it as the ability of the "wisdom of nature to secure so necessary an act of the mind . . ." (ibid., 5:2:67–68). For by this uniform experience we can "infer like effects from like causes . . . [which] is so essential to the subsistence of all human creatures . . ." (ibid.). Such an important function, Hume believed, could not "be trusted to the fallacious deductions of our reason . . ." (ibid.). Rather, "nature has taught us" this principle. "She has implanted in us an instinct" to think properly about unknown causes, even "though we are ignorant of those powers and forces on which this regular course and succession of objects totally depends" (ibid.).

According to Hume, there "is no such thing as *chance* in the world . . ." (ibid., 6:69, emphasis added). However, "our ignorance of the real cause of any event has the same influence [as chance] on our understanding . . ." (ibid.). Hence, we speak of "probabilities" as opposed to "certainties." That is, "there are some cases which are entirely uniform and constant in producing a particular effect, and no instance has ever yet been found of any failure or irregularity in their operation" (ibid., 6:70).

For example, "fire has always burned, and water suffocated, every human creature." And "the production of motion by impulse and gravity is a universal law which has hitherto admitted of no exception" (ibid., 6:70). On the other hand, "there are other causes which have been found more irregular and uncertain, nor has rhubarb always proved a purge, or opium a soporific, to everyone who has taken these medicines." In these latter cases, we have only a probability that the antecedent factor is the real cause. However, when there is without exception a constant conjunction of antecedent and consequent factors, then this uniform experience can be viewed as a "proof." By proof Hume meant "such arguments from experience as leave no room for doubt or opposition" (ibid., 6:2:69, n. 1). Hume, of course, did not believe that this kind of empirical "proof" has the force of a logical demonstration, "for there is no matter of fact which we believe so firmly that we cannot conceive the contrary . . ." (ibid., 5:2:62). On the other hand, if a conjunction has been established by uniform experience then we have no reason to doubt it.

Building on the notion of an empirical "proof" Hume offers what he considers to be a fatal argument against belief in all supernatural intervention in the natural world. "I flatter myself that I have discovered an argument of a like nature which, if just, will, with the wise and learned, be an everlasting check to all kinds of superstitious delusion, and consequently will be useful as long as the world endures . . ." (ibid., 10:1:118).

Just what was Hume's "proof" against miracles? It is uniform experience. A wise man "proportions his belief to the evidence. In such conclusions as are founded on an infallible experience, he expects the event with the last degree of assurance and regards his past experience as a full *proof* of the future existence of that event" (ibid).

Hume explained his point this way: A hundred instances or experiments on one side, and fifty on another, would provide a doubtful expectation of any event. But a hundred uniform experiments, with only one that is contradictory, would reasonably generate a strong degree of assurance (ibid., 119). Hence, it is no miracle that a man, seemingly in good health, should suddenly die, because such a kind of death has been frequently observed to happen (ibid., 122). On the other hand, "it is a miracle that a dead man should come to life, because that has never been observed in any age or country" (ibid.). Therefore, Hume concluded that there must

> be a uniform experience against every miraculous event, otherwise the event would not merit that appellation. And as a uniform experience amounts to a proof, there is here a direct and full *proof*, from the nature of the fact, against the existence of any miracle, nor can such a proof be destroyed or the miracle rendered credible but by an opposite proof which is superior. (Ibid., 122–23)

Just how could Hume be so confident that divine intervention in nature should be disbelieved by all "wise men"? Because "a wise man . . . proportions his belief to the evidence." And such conclusions are founded on "infallible experience" (ibid., 10:1:118). "Uniform experience" in the present is the guide used for concluding what did or did not occur in the past. Without this principle of uniformity between present and past there could be no scientific knowledge of the past. But with the principle of uniformity, argued Hume, there should be no belief in miraculous interruptions of nature.

Whether or not Hume was fully aware of the implication his view of uniformity would have on a scientific understanding of origins is not clear. We do know, however, that Hutton did apply the same logic to geology and concluded that the past history of the earth should be understood in the light of the present natural processes (see chap. 4).

Immanuel Kant (1724–1804)

Kant confessed that he was aroused from his "dogmatic slumbers" by Hume. He accepted Hume's antisupernaturalism and argued that all scientific knowledge must be determined by practical reason which operates according to universal laws. Therefore, it is rationally necessary for us to conclude that miracles never occur (Kant [1793] 1960, 84).

The critical premise is the second one, which claims that practical reason operates according to universal laws. In support of this premise Kant wrote, "In the affairs of life, therefore, it is impossible for us to count on miracles or to take them into consideration at all in our use of reason (and reason must be used in every incident of life)" (ibid., 82).

In brief, miracles are theoretically possible but they are practically impossible. We must live as if they never occur. If we lived any other way it would overthrow the dictates of practical reason and erode the basis of both science and morality, for both science and morality are based on universal principles.

Once more we can see that the key element in the antisupernatural argument is the uniformity or regularity of the operational laws of the universe. Kant believed these regular events to be universal. To deny them by admitting miracles, Kant thought, would be to deny the very basis of a rational and moral life.

Kant reasoned this way: Miracles happen seldom, daily, or never. If they occur daily, then they are not miracles. If they occur seldom then they cannot be observed by reason, which is based on regular natural laws. Hence we must conclude that miracles never occur. Kant insisted "they are *for us*, . . . nothing but natural effects and *ought* never to be adjudged otherwise. . . . To venture beyond these limits is rashness and immodesty . . ." (ibid., 84, emphasis added).

Here again there is the recognition that natural laws by nature are manifest in uniformly observed regularities in nature. Without uniformity there is no science, but with uniformity there are no supernatural explanations.

Antony Flew

In his article on "Miracles" in *The Encyclopedia of Philosophy*, Flew notes that "Hume was primarily concerned, not with the question of fact, but with that of evidence. The problem was how the occurrence of a miracle could be proved, rather than whether any such events had ever occurred." However, adds Flew, "our sole ground for characterizing the reported occurrence as miraculous is at the same time a sufficient reason for calling it physically impossible." Why is this so?

Because "the critical historian, confronted with some story of a miracle, will usually dismiss it out of hand. . . ." On what grounds? Flew answers, "To justify his procedure he will have to appeal to precisely the principle which Hume advanced: the 'absolute impossibility or miraculous nature' of the events attested must, 'in the eyes of all reasonable people . . . alone be regarded as a sufficient refutation.'"

In short, even though miracles are not logically impossible, they are scientifically impossible. "For it is only and precisely by presuming that the laws that hold today held in the past . . . that we can rationally interpret the *detritus* [fragments] of the past as evidence and from it construct our account of what actually happened" (Edwards 1967, 5:346–53).

Flew's argument against the supernatural can be summarized this way:

1. Miracles are by nature particular and unrepeatable.
2. Natural events are by nature general and repeatable.
3. Now, in practice, the evidence for the general and repeatable is always greater than that for the particular and unrepeatable.
4. Therefore, in practice, the evidence against miracles will always be greater than the evidence for them.

The key to Flew's argument is the third premise, that the regular or repeatable counts as greater evidence. For science by its very nature is not based on the exceptional or the odd but on the normal and the usual. Here again, uniformity is the key to science, and uniformity argues against supernatural intervention into the operations of nature.

Alastair McKinnon

Another contemporary thinker has offered arguments with similar premises against allowing the supernatural in science. McKinnon's argument can be summarized as follows:

1. A scientific law is a generalization based on observation.
2. Any exception to a scientific law invalidates that law as such and calls for a revision of it.
3. A miracle is an exception to a scientific law.
4. Therefore, a miracle would call for a revision of a law and the

recognition of a broader law, which thereby explains the "miracle" as a natural event (Geisler 1982b, 52).

Here the critical premise is the second one. It is admitted readily that a scientific law is a generalization based on observation. But a miracle is by nature an exceptional event, and thus the miraculous can play no part in science. Hence, one can be a creationist and a scientist at the same time, but there is no such thing as a scientific view of creation. This is as impossible as there being a supernaturally natural event or a miraculous natural occurrence.

Patrick Nowell-Smith

One of the most forceful arguments against the compatibility of science and the belief in supernatural events is that of Nowell-Smith. In his famous essay on "Miracles" (Flew and MacIntyre 1955) he writes, "We may believe [the supernaturalist] when he says that no scientific method or hypothesis known to him will explain it." But "to say that it is inexplicable as a result of natural agents is already beyond his competence as a scientist, and to say that it must be ascribed to supernatural agents is to say something that no one could possibly have the right to affirm on the evidence alone" (ibid., 245–46).

Nowell-Smith further insists that "no matter how strange an event someone reports, the statement that it must have been due to a supernatural agent cannot be a part of that report" (ibid., 246). The reason for this derives from the fact "that no scientist can at present explain certain phenomena." But "it does not follow that the phenomena are inexplicable by scientific methods, still less that they must be attributed to supernatural agents" (ibid., 247). For "there is still the possibility that science may be able, in the future, to offer an explanation which, though couched in quite new terms, remains strictly scientific" (ibid., 248).

A good example of this is the fact that for many years it was held that the flight of the bumblebee was unexplainable by natural law. However, the principles of this natural occurrence have come to light in the discovery of cellular power packs called mitochondria. These natural power packs make possible the rapid wing motion that produces flight. This discovery illustrates the folly of insisting that a presently unexplained event must be caused by a supernatural agent.

What then is a scientific explanation? According to Nowell-Smith, "a scientific explanation is an hypothesis from which *prediction* can be made, which can afterwards be verified" (ibid., 249, emphasis added). In addition, "an explanation must explain *how* an event comes about; otherwise it is simply a learned . . . name for the phenomenon to be explained." In view of this definition, "if miracles are 'lawful' it should be possible to state the laws; if not, the alleged explanation amounts to a confession that they are inexplicable." For "if we can detect any order in God's interventions it should be possible to extrapolate in the usual way and to predict when and how a miracle will occur. . . . otherwise the hypothesis is not open either to confirmation or refutation" (ibid., 251).

Nowell-Smith concludes with a challenge to a supernaturalist:

> Let him consider the meaning of the word 'explanation' and let him ask himself whether this notion does not involve that of a law or hypothesis capable of predictive expansion. And then let him ask himself whether such an explanation would not be natural, in whatever terms it was couched, and how the notion of 'the supernatural' could play any part in it. (Ibid., 253)

If the supernaturalist should object that he is simply redefining the "natural" to include miracles, Nowell-Smith replies:

> I do not wish to quarrel about words. I will concede your supernatural, if this is all that it means. For the supernatural will be nothing but a new field for scientific inquiry, a field as different from physics as physics is from psychology, but not differing in principle or requiring any non-scientific method. (Ibid., 253)

We may now summarize the argument this way:

1. Only what has predictive capabilities can qualify as an explanation of an event.
2. A miracle has no predictive capabilities.
3. Therefore, a miracle does not qualify as an explanation of any event.

The long and short of Nowell-Smith's discussion is that only natural explanations can qualify as scientific explanations, since only natural explanations have predictive capabilities. Why? Because natural laws are based on regularities (not singularities). And, as Hume argued, regular or uniform conjunction can be used to make predictions about the future as well as what some have called "retrodictions" about the past. But the supernatural singularities have no such predictive or retrodictive powers. Therefore, according to Nowell-Smith, positing a supernatural creation has no place in science.

A Creationist Response to Purely Naturalistic Approaches to Origin Science

There are several reasons why the purely naturalistic approach to origins fails to make a definitive case for limiting all science (including that of origins) to a consideration of purely natural (secondary) causes. One of the most important is the failure to recognize the unique nature of the study of origin singularities in contrast to the regularities of operation science (see chap. 1).

The Confusion of Origin Science and Operation Science

Early scientists, such as Bacon, Kepler, Newton, and Kelvin, implied a difference between the origin of the universe (and/or life) and the operation of the universe. They believed that the former had a supernatural (primary) cause, but they limited natural (secondary) causes to the latter. To be sure, subsequent creationists sometimes attributed anomalies in the operation of the universe to supernatural causes. But the fact that creationists occasionally interjected supernatural causes into their study of the operation of the universe does not justify noncreationists projecting natural causes for the origin of the universe (and/or life).

The creationist is wrong in positing a supernatural cause for any regular repeated event in nature, for a regularly recurring pattern of events necessitates a natural explanation. But singularities do not necessitate a natural cause. Thus the naturalist is unjustified in assuming all irregular (or singular) events have natural (secondary) causes. But since the events of origin are unique and unrepeated, they do not, as such, come under the domain of operation science and thus may have a supernatural cause.

It is the fact that origin science deals with singularities which make predictions impossible. No trend can be read from a singularity, that is, from a solitary event which forms no part of a recurring pattern of events. In fact, origin science as such, whether creation or macro-evolution, does not deal with a prediction but with a kind of retro-diction. That is, it is a forensic look backward toward a past singularity from which no particular conclusion can be drawn about any future creative events.

Misapplication of the Principle of Uniformity (Analogy)

There is a crucial difference between uniformitarianism and the principle of uniformity. Uniformitarianism assumes that all past causes will be natural ones like those observed in nature at the present. This is not a scientific assertion, but a philosophical one. That is, this kind of uniformitarianism is not justified by observations of a repeated pattern of events in the present. Rather, it is a meta-physical speculation which goes well beyond the domain of opera-tion science. Such uniformitarianism is not science but scientism. It is not the scientific study of nature; it is philosophical naturalism.

In fact, at the basis of such uniformitarianism is the principle of continuity, that there is a continuous, unbroken series of physical causes. This view is now challenged by the big bang theory which posits a radical discontinuity at the very beginning of the physical universe. Indeed, in view of quantum physics, the older determinism has yielded to a probabilism which recognizes the possibility of divine intervention. In view of this, even some atheists are reluctantly admitting that supernatural intervention into the natural order of causes is possible. As one atheist put it:

> Distressing as it is for an atheist such as myself to have to admit it, we have here a model for God's interference, by way of miracle, with the working out of ordinary natural processes. It is tempting to argue that, if God can overrule physical necessitations, then they are not really *necessitations* after all. But a physical necessitation does not cease to be a necessitation just because the effect will fail to occur if God inter-feres. God's inaction in ordinary circumstances is not an extra causal factor in the situation: the physical cause is then the *total* cause. But if God does interfere, then the determinations of his will become part of a new total cause necessitating a different effect. (Armstrong 1978, 156)

In contrast to naturalistic uniformitarianism, the principle of uni-formity simply says that "the present is the key to the past." That is, it affirms some kind of analogy between present and past which is not limited to secondary causes. For example, the science of archaeology (as Lyell acknowledged) uses the principle of uniformity to posit primary (intelligent) causes in the past. It argues that since it takes an intelligent cause to make a sculpture in the present, we can (by analogy) assume that similar sculptures from the past had similar intelligent causes.

This, to be sure, does not prove that all primary (intelligent) causes must be supernatural (see appendix 2). But neither is there any scientific ground for ruling out the possibility that an intelligent primary cause posited for origins (on the basis of uniformly observed conjunctions) could be a supernatural one. Hence, the door is still open for a creationist to posit a supernatural cause for the origin of the universe and/or life. Of course, there is no physical analogy in the present of an ex nihilo creation of the universe.* However, origin science is also based on the principle of causality, which says that every event has an adequate cause. Hence, there is no reason that the event of the universe coming into being should be exempt from this principle, even though we have no observable physical analogy to it in the present. Indeed, since ex nihilo creation entails the coming into existence of the physical universe (with all its forces and laws), there obviously was no prior physical (or natural) cause. Hence, it would be necessary by the very nature of the case that the cause be nonphysical and nonnatural. Thus the principle of uniformity (analogy) would support a supernatural cause, not eliminate it as uniformitarians suppose.

The Confusion of Regular Basis and Singular Object

All science, whether about past or present events, is based on uniformly observed patterns or causal conjunctions. As Hume rightly observed, without uniformity there would be no way of knowing anything beyond the immediate. Thus origin science and operation science both depend on a repeatedly observed conjunction of a particular kind of event with a certain kind of cause. This is why the principle of uniformity (analogy) is necessary for a scientific understanding of the past. For without knowledge from present observation

---

*There are however some mental analogies to ex nihilo creation, such as "conjuring up a mental image" or "conceiving a new idea," as it were "out of nothing."

that certain kinds of effects are produced by certain kinds of causes (and others are not), there would be no way to know what kinds of causes to posit for singularities or unrepeated events from the past. In short, present regularities (i.e., constant conjunctions) are the basis for getting at past singularities.

The forensic scientist depends on uniformity. For without assuming that constant conjunctions of the present also held in the past, he could not reconstruct the crime. Since the killing occurred only once and cannot be repeated, the forensic scientist must assume that similar situations in the present (which can be simulated repeatedly) are the key to understanding what probably happened in this past event which cannot be repeated. The same is true in archaeology. When one comes upon a past singularity (like the great pyramids of Egypt), he must use his observational knowledge from repeated (or repeatable) instances in the present in order to posit the likely cause of this singularity in the past.

Macroevolution is another case in point. It is not occurring in the present, nor can these large changes be reproduced in a lab. It is a past singularity which is not being repeated (in nature or the lab) in the present. Nonetheless, macroevolution is still a valid scientific approach to the origin of species. This is true so long as it is based on presently observed (or observable) causal conjunctions of small changes in a short time. These can then be projected to imply large changes over long periods in the past. So while origin science is *based on* present repeatable events, it is nevertheless *about* past unrepeated events. Thus the *basis* of macroevolution must be regularity, while the *object* is a singularity.

This same reasoning applies whether the cause posited is a secondary cause (such as natural law) or a primary cause (such as an intelligent being). For example, if those in search of extraterrestrial intelligence (SETI) receive a message from outer space, they will be justified in positing an intelligent source for it. By analogy with many messages known in the present to have come from intelligent beings, they can legitimately posit an intelligent cause of a similar message from space. In short, the *basis* of speculation about singular events is repeated observation of causal connection, even though the *object* is a single event. This is how origin science works, whether for evolution or for creation.

In view of this point, the error of Hume's naturalism becomes evident. He rightly saw that knowledge about the past must be *based on* a regularity (constant conjunction). But he wrongly assumed that the *object* of our knowledge cannot be a singularity. But what Hume did not see, William Paley did point out in his famous design argument. For Paley saw that uniform experience (of constant conjunction) always yields an intelligent cause, not a purely natural law, for a complex order such as a watch. In apparent agreement with Hume's argument about constant conjunction as the basis for knowledge about past events, Paley wrote:

> Wherever we see marks of contrivance, we are led for its cause to an *intelligent* author. And this transition of the understanding is founded upon *uniform experience*. We see intelligence constantly contriving; that is, we see intelligence *constantly producing* effects, marked and distinguished by certain properties—not certain particular properties, but by a kind and class of properties, such as relation to an end, relation of parts to one another and to a common purpose. We see, wherever we are witnesses to the actual formation of things, nothing except intelligence producing effects so marked and distinguished in the same manner. We wish to account for their *origin*. Our experience suggests a cause perfectly adequate to this account. No experience, no single instance or example, can be offered in favor of any other. In this cause, therefore, we ought to rest; in this cause the common sense of mankind has, in fact, rested, because it agrees with that which in all cases is the foundation of knowledge—the *undeviating course of their experience*. ([1802] 1963, 37, emphasis added)

So, contrary to popular opinion, Hume did not refute Paley's design argument in advance. In fact, we suggest the reverse is true. For there is uniform experience that only an intelligent cause produces the kind of specified complexity found in living organisms (see chap. 7). And to argue, in spite of this, that it is possible that Webster's unabridged dictionary resulted from an explosion in a printing shop, is to reject the principle of uniformity (which is based on constant conjunction). For uniform experience reveals that an intelligent cause regularly produces that kind of complex information (see chap. 7). To posit a nonintelligent natural cause based on rare occurrences or minute probabilities is not science; it is luck. And it is subject to Hume's devastating critique against believing in such rare events without any real basis in constant conjunction. Therefore, contrary to widely prevailing opinion, Hume's argument does not destroy the credibility of supposing there is supernatural intervention in the world; it actually supports it.

Summary and Conclusion

Scientific speculation about the past is based on the principle of uniformity (or analogy). The present is the key to the past. What we observe to be constantly conjoined in the present we can assume to be constantly conjoined in the past. Since Hume's day it has been common to assume that the principle of uniformity excludes all reference to supernatural primary causes. However, this is not necessarily the case. For whereas operation science is limited to natural (secondary) causes for a regular pattern of events, this is not necessarily so of origin science which deals with singularities. All that is needed for one to legitimately posit an intelligent cause for some past singularity is to show that similar events in the present can be constantly conjoined to an intelligent cause. As long as the *basis* for the forensic reconstruction of the past event is some regularly observable causal conjunction, the *object* of this speculation can be an unrepeated singularity. As we shall see in the next chapters, the origin of life is a past singularity which allows a creationist explanation based on observations in the present which indicate that this kind of event can be produced by an intelligent cause.

6

New Possibilities
for a Creationist View
of Origins

From the very beginning of modern science there was a wide-spread belief in a supernatural cause (creator) of the origin of the universe and of living things (see chap. 2). But this belief in a primary cause of origins faded in significance as stress shifted to *how* God operated in his creation through secondary causes. Eventually, operation science co-opted the territory of origin science (see chaps. 3–4). There were many reasons for this shift.

The Fall of Origin Science

Reasons for the Decline of Origin Science

One reason behind the decline of origin science was that scientists in the seventeenth century rejected the notion of final causes in nature. These men were interested in learning by experience *how* the world works, not *why* it exists and what higher purposes might be involved. The study of teleology (purpose) was relegated to the realm of theology and philosophy. It was not in vogue to consider final or efficient causes. The tendency to discard the need for an efficient cause (producer) with the final cause (purpose) was no doubt accelerated by the fact that Aristotle, whose physics was also rejected, had identified the creator of the world as a final cause (Aristotle 1941, 880–84).

Furthermore, early modern scientists reasoned that a created nature must be contingent, having its structure impressed upon it by the Creator. This view necessitated a change in the methodology or approach to nature from that used by the Greeks. In the seventeenth century a Greek view of reality dominated the intellectual world. An essential facet of Greek science was that the world is a living organism impregnated with divinity and final causes. After basic principles were derived, then particular truths of the world could be arrived at by deduction. Experiment was practiced, but with the intent of illustrating what was already known rather than learning something new. Greek experiment was more along the lines of laboratory demonstration. The paradigm of Greek science was Euclidean geometry, a purely mental exercise in which sensory experience has no essential role. But with the decline of the Greek view of science went also the search for a first cause.

Third, the newly emerging modern science stressed the orderly way the Creator (primary Cause) works in his creation—that is, through secondary (natural) causes. As scientists succeeded in discovering these natural causes, they felt increasingly confident about applying these principles to questions of origin. At the same time they recognized that it was an error to explain that the operation of the universe resulted from a supernatural cause. Scientists gradually failed to perceive a need to consider a primary cause.

Fourth, even when there was recognition that science about the past is different from science about the present (as the distinction between cosmogony and cosmology implies), nevertheless there seemed to be little or no appreciation of the difference between singularity science and regularity science (see introduction). It was generally assumed that origin events came under the same category as regularly recurring events. Science became totally preoccupied with the study of secondary causes.

Results of the Decline of Origin Science

Seventeenth- and eighteenth-century science, like the society in which it flourished, was preoccupied with certainty. As a result, in the scientific method attention was given to verification. An experiment that worked was likely to be construed as proving or verifying the truth of a theory. By contrast, in the twentieth century scientists have increasingly emphasized the falsifiability, not the verifiability, of a theory. If a theory is false it can in principle be shown to be false by empirical test measured against recurrent events.

Despite significant theistic influences on science, scientists were acutely aware that authoritarian religious control can stifle inquiry, and they sought to be free of such influence. In order to avoid the charge that they were making science religious, early scientists sorely needed a way to legitimately handle the connection between their belief in a creator and the new science. Their hope for insuring their freedom was the scientific method, which emphasized observation and experiment rather than authority, whether religious or philosophical. The new method of science appeared to have a degree of philosophical neutrality connected with it. Theists and naturalists were united in their conviction that the proper way to gain knowledge of nature was through investigation of secondary causes, for these are the continuously acting causes in regular events.

In restricting the scope of inquiry to recurring events of nature, operation science provided a way to have confidence that one's inquiry was not trespassing on divine territory. In operation science one was dealing with secondary causes to explain regular events. Appeals to the God-hypothesis to "solve" some particularly knotty problem of the ongoing operation of the universe was considered quite out of bounds. A scientist would grapple with some anomaly, believing that behind the apparent chaos of events was a true order imposed by the Creator. Operation science was a diligent search to discover the pattern, rule, or law behind the events. What this means, of course, is that an assumption about nature was being implicitly made. Early scientists believed that in the general regularity of nature, physical events recur. It was a conviction that was ingrained in the European mind for centuries.

In other words, the view of nature as a pattern of recurrent events is a central feature that makes modern operation science what it is. It was not merely that nature was viewed as dynamic; a flux is dynamic. Modern scientists held an implicit faith that at bottom the flux was only apparent, that a pattern of recurrent events lay behind it. Although post-Kantian scientists questioned whether the pattern really exists in our minds and can be imposed on the flux in our construction of theories, it is clear the early scientists believed the pattern was objectively there to be found in nature. Operation science was simply the search for that pattern.

Rejection of the God-of-the-Gaps View

Because of the Christian influence in the rise of operation science there has been a tendency on the part of some scientists to answer a perplexing scientific question or fill in some gap in our knowledge by stating that God directly intervenes in nature. This is known fittingly as the God-of-the-gaps view.

There is legitimate concern about applying the God-hypothesis in operation science. A classic example of this approach to scientific problem-solving is seen in the life of the great Isaac Newton, who appealed to the God-hypothesis to account for certain anomalies in the heavens. Later, Pierre Simon de Laplace discovered natural causes that accounted for such discrepancies. This was an important but painful lesson for scientists to learn. This is illustrated by the story about Napoleon, who asked Laplace why God was absent from his analysis. To this Laplace responded, "Sire, I have no need of that hypothesis." Although some have misunderstood Laplace's reply in this instance as being anti-God, it was in keeping with the belief that operation science should be limited to natural causes. Laplace's answer to Napoleon has since become the paradigm response of the scientific community to the question of the God-hypothesis in operation science.

Exclusive Use of Secondary Causes

The success of operation science, using exclusively secondary causes, brought scientists a sense of mastery over nature that was unknown in all previous history. They began developing a method of compartmentalized thinking that would eventually influence all of European society. These men believed that science is limited to secondary causes; only religion and philosophy may appeal to primary causes. Considering the questioning nature of man it could be anticipated that someone would attempt to extend the methods of operation science to seek answers to the great questions of origin.

This process began with Descartes, who talked mostly of operation science. But he entered the speculative area of origins, which his predecessors had assumed did not have a secondary or mechanical cause. To avoid the charge of being out of step with the religious sensibilities of his time Descartes showed only hypothetically how the world might have formed by pure natural causes without God. Thus Descartes opened the door to the modern naturalistic approach to origins (see chap. 2).

Following Descartes were Buffon, Kant, and Laplace in astronomy, Hutton and Lyell in geology, and Darwin in biology (see chaps. 3–4).

These pioneers of origin science used secondary causes and the principle of uniformity to explain how certain things in the past might have happened. Although the new science of origin studies capitalized on the momentum of using secondary causes in operation science, it was noticed by some that this method, as applied to singular events, was in a different category of investigation. Recognition of the methodological differences in astronomy led to giving names appropriate to the subject matter. The term *cosmology* (operation science) denoted study of the ongoing, regular operation of the universe. Principles of cosmology can be tested empirically. The word *cosmogony*, however, suggested a different domain of study, the origin of the universe, solar system, and planets. These singular events can be speculated about, and hypotheses of origin can be offered.

The Revival of Origin Science: Aspects That Influence Its Renewal

The distinction between cosmology and cosmogony was part of early science. This went into decline with the advent of atomic theory in the nineteenth century. (Atoms were held to be indestructible, indivisible, discrete units of matter that were neither created nor destroyed [the first law of thermodynamics].) Thereafter the term *cosmogony* became an embarrassment. The term is still used today, even though the distinction between it and cosmology has tended to blur. The distinction, however, is valid and has remained latent in the scientific endeavor.

In fact, scientists who studied origins proceeded to develop plausible scenarios of events. (For example, they attempted to explain how, given certain minimal conditions, the solar system might have formed.) They relied on their knowledge of secondary causes and the principle of uniformity, and also used a modified scientific method which kept hypothetical issues consistent with known principles of operation science. In this way their hypotheses could be considered scientific.

This gives rise to another important distinction, that between the *object* of a scientific inquiry and the *basis* for it. The object of inquiry may be either regular or singular events. But the basis for such inquiries can only be regular conjunctions, as David Hume so forcefully argued (see chap. 5). Origin events are singular, and although they may be the object of scientific inquiry, they can never be the basis for investigation. Thus origin science is capable of dealing with past unobserved singularities. In this way it is distinct from operation science, which deals only with regularities. Origin science is a singularity science about the past, rather than a regularity science which deals with a recurring pattern of events.

A Forensic Science

The investigation of origins may be compared to researching an unwitnessed murder. Clues can be pieced together to give a plausible reconstruction of what occurred. But the reconstructed scenario is still speculation, no matter how plausible it is.

Because a murder (or origin) does not recur, hypotheses about it cannot be empirically tested. We may re-enact the crime (or origin) and test the reconstruction or model against data collected in experiments. But we cannot test our model against the original event. There is thus no direct way to know whether the results from these experiments give information about the particular unique event in question. Origin science then functions more like a forensic science than an empirical science.

A Place for Primary Causes

Operation scientists succeeded in discovering secondary causes and understanding the operation of the universe. This success led them to apply similar principles to origin questions. Nature was conceived of as a continuous web of natural (secondary) causes and effects. Primary causes were interpreted as having no intervening role in the ongoing processes of nature. The reasoning went like this: If nature is a seamless web in which God does not interfere, then it must be that natural causes account for the beginning; secondary causes extend back further and further until the beginning. This, scientists believed, would give a true scientific explanation of origins (see chaps. 2–5).

The modern search for the beginning, however, has turned into a nightmare. Astrophysicist Robert Jastrow tells the story in *God and the Astronomers*: "For the scientist who has lived by his faith in the power of reason, the story ends like a bad dream" (1978, 105). A scientist who is committed to philosophical naturalism finds it difficult to accept that the data indicate a beginning of the universe. Philosophical naturalism has implicit within it the notion that there never was a beginning. So, for example, the steady state hypothesis which denied a beginning had an intuitive appeal to committed naturalists. The strange thing is that even when scientists have looked through a naturalistic lens, the data still seemed to point to a beginning. This seems to be an instance where in spite of a naturalistic bias the door was opened to a supernatural explanation. For the notion of a beginning has theistic implications, including the possibility of a primary supernatural cause. This has undoubtedly troubled many committed naturalists; hence the "bad dream" Jastrow referred to.

Contemporary approaches to the origin of the universe have taken a radical turn with the widespread acceptance of a big bang cosmogony. According to Jastrow, "Three lines of evidence—the motions of the galaxies, the laws of thermodynamics, and the life story of the stars—pointed to one conclusion: all indicated that the Universe had a beginning" (ibid., 111). In short, "science has proven that the Universe exploded into being at a certain moment" (ibid., 114). Thus "the scientist's pursuit of the past ends in the moment of creation" (ibid., 115).

Although some scientists believe the big bang is only the most recent explosion in an endless series of explosions and contractions, a current body of evidence supports the scientific model of a beginning of the universe. The second law of thermodynamics affirms that in a closed isolated system (such as the whole universe) the amount of usable energy is decreasing. So it is argued that even if the universe did have enough mass to rebound, nevertheless, like a bouncing ball in reverse, it would rebound less and less until it could rebound no more. Thus, according to big bang cosmogony, the regular laws of the universe (thermodynamics, measurable expansion) point to a unique singular beginning.

Whether or not the big bang theory is correct is not the point here. What is significant is that a scientific hypothesis has been developed in which the regularities of the present are used as a key to formulating a scientific view suggesting a past singularity of origin. Without these observable laws there would be no way to construct a scientific model about a past unobserved singularity. So regularities (constant conjunctions) in the present are the key to a scientific approach to this singularity in the past. By using observed regularities from the present it is possible to construct a scientific model about a past singularity which has no parallel in the present.

Most scientists have acknowledged the scientific plausibility of the big bang hypothesis. However, it is an example of origin science. For by using the principles of causality and uniformity one can make a plausible case in support of a particular view about the singularity of the origin of the universe. Observed regular events of the present (such as the second law of thermodynamics), which can be described by known law, can aid in understanding an unobserved singular event of the past. And if this is so, then it is possible to posit a primary cause for the origin of the universe.

Some Key Differences Between Origin Science and Operation Science

Origin science does not involve an unbroken continuity of causes. For the scientific evidence points to a beginning of the universe. And if there was a beginning then the need to seek an endless series of causes is gone. As Jastrow aptly put it,

> Astronomers now find they have painted themselves into a corner because they have proven, by their own methods, that the world began abruptly in an act of creation to which you can trace the seeds of every star, every planet, every living thing in this cosmos and on the earth. And they have found that all this happened as a product of forces they cannot hope to discover. (1982, 15)

One reason scientists are surprised that uniform laws point to a singular beginning is that there has been such a widespread confusion of operation science and origin science. They failed to keep in mind that only the *operation* of the universe, not its *origin*, demands regularity. Only the *basis* for science needs to be a constant conjunction or regularity; its *object* can be a singularity. In short, they did not recognize the difference between a scientific analysis of singularities and that of regularities.

So the big bang theory of the origin of the universe has brought into sharp focus the need to clearly distinguish between the cause of origin and the cause of operation of the universe. This only reminds us of the distinction between cosmogony (study of origin of the cosmos) and cosmology (study of the operation of the cosmos). Both are legitimate studies. Hence, while scientists rightly rule miracles out of regularity science, of which operation science is the application in the present (see chap. 5), they cannot thereby eliminate them from singularity science, of which origin science is an application to the past. The supernatural is correctly ruled out of operation science because operation science is based on regular events which must have secondary causes. Because origins, like miracles (see appendix 3), are singularities, it remains possible that a primary cause was involved. Indeed, according to the big bang hypothesis, no regularly observed causes operative in the world were involved in the origin of the universe. Hence, the big bang model illustrates that a discontinuity at the moment of beginning can be a legitimate characteristic of origin science.

Jastrow notes that not all scientists were happy with the conclusion that the universe had a beginning. Arthur Stanley Eddington wrote (1931), "The notion of a beginning is repugnant to me . . . I simply do not believe that the present order of things started off with a bang . . ." (Jastrow 1978, 112). Walter Nernst said, "To deny the infinite duration of time would be to betray the very foundations of science." More recently Phillip Morrison of MIT said, "I find it hard to accept the Big Bang theory; I would *like* to reject it" (ibid., 113, emphasis added). Allan Sandage of Palomar Observatory once said, "It is such a strange conclusion . . . it cannot really be true" (ibid., 113).

Why did scientists react in this unusual and unscientific way to the mounting evidence for a radical and singular beginning of our universe? Jastrow offers this response:

> I think part of the answer is that scientists cannot bear the thought of a natural phenomenon which cannot be explained, even with unlimited time and money. There is a kind of religion in science; it is the religion of a person who believes there is order and harmony in the Universe. Every event can be explained in a rational way as the product of some previous event; every effect must have its cause; there is no First Cause. (Ibid., 113)

But in spite of the fact that many scientists find the results of the scientific evidence for a singular beginning of the universe to be undesirable, nevertheless the scientific evidence is strong that there was a beginning of the universe. Indeed it results from following the principle of uniformity, which is the key to understanding the past. Thus unexpectedly the principle of uniformity has led to a break in the scientific community with the long-standing principle of endless continuity. And with this break, the door has been reopened for origin science.

In view of this development we suggest that just as applying secondary causes to astronomical explanations of origin opened the door to the decline of a special creationist view, so the big bang theory of the origin of the universe has resurrected the possibility of a creationist view of origins in astronomy. Likewise, just as a secondary cause was extended from astronomy to geology and biology, there is now no reason why a primary-cause explanation of origins cannot be applied in these areas to re-establish a creationist view. In short, it appears that while in the nineteenth century the application of secondary causes moved from astronomy to geology and biology, thus leading to the decline of creationist views, now the plausibility of a primary cause for the origin of the universe can be extended from astronomy to geology and biology,* thus reopening the door for a special creationist view.

The Possibility of a Primary Supernatural Cause

An important lesson that origin science learned from big bang cosmogony is that the principle of continuity does not apply to origin science either. Thus the universe may have a primary cause. For one cannot demand on purely scientific grounds that there is an endless series of physical causes. This is especially so in view of the scientific evidence which points to a beginning of the physical series of causes.

Further, the primary cause may be a supernatural cause. Science is based on the principle of causality: every event has an adequate cause. This means that the scientific evidence for the big bang leaves open the possibility of a primary cause of the origin of the cosmos. For the scientific evidence points to a beginning of the natural (space-time) world. And if every event needs an adequate cause, then it naturally suggests a primary cause of the beginning of the universe. As Jastrow put it, many scientists were surprised "by the discovery that the world had a beginning under conditions in which the known

---

*Actually, discontinuity has always existed in the fossil record, as evolutionists from Darwin to Gould have acknowledged (see chap. 7). So in this sense the big bang cosmology is only the occasional cause which enables scientists to view anew what has always been there in the fossil record. The difference between evolutionist and creationist perspectives is a matter not of facts but of interpretation.

laws of physics are not valid, and as a product of forces or circumstances we cannot discover" (ibid., 113–14). Jastrow even went so far as to say "that there are what I or anyone would call supernatural forces at work is now, I think, a scientifically proven fact" (1982, 18).

To be sure, not all scientists understand "supernatural" to mean a creator. Some simply look at it as a "mystery." Be that as it may, at least current theory in astronomy has opened the door for considering a possible primary cause of the origin of the universe. That is, it is conceivable in origin science to consider a primary cause that is beyond the physical universe and independent of it, and that produced singularities such as bringing the physical universe into existence. Despite his self-proclaimed agnosticism, even Jastrow acknowledges what he calls the "theistic" implications of his speculative scenario of origins (ibid., 17).

So in big-bang cosmogony there is a singularity for which it is valid to posit an unknown, unobserved primary force to account for it. Of course this scientific evidence for a beginning does not in itself make it necessary to conclude there is a primary cause of the material universe. One could simply posit that the material universe began, but without a cause. As Anthony Kenny put it, "According to the big bang theory, the whole matter of the universe began to exist at a particular time in the remote past. A proponent of such a theory, at least if he is an atheist, must believe that the matter of the universe came from nothing and by nothing" (1969, 66).

Such a view would kill operation science as well as origin science, for it is inherently irrational to suppose events occur willy-nilly without a cause. In response we note that even Hume said, "I never asserted so absurd a proposition as that anything might arise without a cause" (1932, 1:187). Likewise, Laplace believed it was absurd to assume "an event without a cause" ([1814] 1951, 16). Indeed the whole of modern science from Bacon on is based on the search for adequate causes of events.

So this well-established scientific practice of positing an adequate cause of an event leads to positing a cause of the beginning of the whole physical universe. Thus the big bang hypothesis in origin science illustrates that one can have a scientific approach to understanding singularities and discontinuities, and also that a primary cause is possible.

There is, of course, historic precedent for positing a primary supernatural cause of the universe. As we have seen earlier, Bacon, Kepler,

Newton, Kelvin, and others all believed the evidence of the universe pointed to a primary cause which they believed to be supernatural (see chap. 2). Newton said clearly,

> It is not to be conceived that mere mechanical causes could give birth to so many regular motions, since the comets range over all parts of the heavens in very eccentric orbits; for by that kind of motion they pass easily through the orbs of the planets, and with great rapidity; and in their aphelions, where they move the slowest, are detained the longest, they recede to the greatest distances from each other, and hence suffer the least disturbance from their mutual attractions. This most beautiful system of the sun, planets, and comets, could only proceed from the counsel and dominion of an intelligent and powerful Being. ([1687] n.d., 369)

Of course, these early scientists were theistic or deistic (see chap. 2). Hence, they had no difficulty seeing the evidence pointing to a creator. Unfortunately, as the one-category-for-science view developed, any mention of a primary cause was considered philosophical speculation or religion.

Rejection of One Category for Science

It was acknowledged in the early days of modern science that the subject matter determines the instrument used in inquiry. That is why astronomers observe stars with a telescope instead of a microscope. Similarly it was determined that the method of inquiry into nature must inform us about nature, and not reflect our own ideas about nature. In other words, scientists must have a check on their speculations and hypotheses about nature. What modern scientists needed and in fact developed was a way to empirically test hypotheses about nature. Such hypotheses are checked against the recurring events of nature, thus eliminating false or wrong ideas. Other hypotheses are confirmed or verified. Of course, early scientists made mistakes in this approach and falsely concluded that verified hypotheses were absolutely true. Over the years operation science has proved to be a self-correcting process. In time scientists learned that their views about verification were mistaken. This scientific method became refined over time, and the great success of operation science is a testimony to the validity of its method.

An example of this is that Johannes Kepler discarded one grand theory of planetary motion for another. Why? Because his hypothesis based on circular motion had been falsified by Tycho Brahe's accurate data about the recurrent planetary motion. It was to the credit of Kepler that he abandoned his earlier hypothesis. Kepler's diligent search was rewarded when he used elliptical orbits in his model.

If we recognize that it is inappropriate to investigate stars with a microscope, why insist on applying operation-science criteria to non-recurring, singular-origin events? The method of choice must fit the object under investigation. Origin events cannot be repeated for empirical test. Investigators of origin science should use principles which fit the object of their enquiry, such as the principles of causality and uniformity (analogy). Origin science deals with past singularities, for which these principles are particularly appropriate.

Newton and other early scientists were preoccupied with discovering the operational laws of the universe (see chaps. 3–4). Hence, they did not stress or develop the principles of origin science. Indeed, Newton even violated the principles of operation science by saying God intervened to correct the operational orbits of the planets. However, this mistake in the area of operation science did not invalidate the legitimacy of Newton positing a primary cause to explain the origin of the universe. The validity of positing a primary cause, however, has not been recognized because the one-category-for-science view has dominated intellectual thought. Operation science deals with only secondary causes; it seemed logical for scientists to call any mention of primary causes metaphysics, or at least non-science. However, simply because the universe *operates* by natural causes does not mean that it *originated* that way. Likewise, we may know the principles of how a machine operates, but this does not show how the machine began. Michael Polanyi demonstrated that the operation of a machine is independent of the machine's origin, which can only result from intelligent shaping. Might this also be true for the grandest machine of all, the universe?

A Distinction Between Final Cause and Efficient Cause

Following Aristotle, medieval scientists often associated the primary (first) cause with teleology or final causality, rather than with an efficient cause. Hence, when Aristotelian teleology in science came into disrepute, the "baby" (of efficient [primary] causality) was thrown out with the "bathwater" (of final causality). This seems to be one of the reasons that the recognition and development of the legitimacy of primary causes in origin science has been so long in coming. For scientists who do not clearly distinguish origin science from operation science tend to absorb the former into the latter. At any rate, since teleology (final causality) is not formally involved in the idea of a first (efficient) cause, the way is now clear for exploring the use of primary causes in the domain of origin science without thereby getting science entangled in the debate about purpose.

A *Recognition of Arguments from Analogy*

In order to show a scientific connection between cause and effect one need not have either identical effects or identical causes but only similar ones. Technically no two space-time events are identical. As A. David Kline noted, "No event occurs twice" (1983, 40), for they occur at different times and places. Hence, all events will at best be only similar. In view of this some scientists speak of event types that are confirmed by observation (ibid.). What is repeated, then, is not the event but a similar pattern of events. As a consequence, all arguments comparing events are arguments from analogy. Broadly speaking, this is what uniformity means, namely, past causes are assumed to have been analogous to presently observed ones. More precisely uniformity (analogy) entails that the kind of causes known to produce a certain kind of event in the present probably produced similar kinds of events in the past.

Hence, we need not expect that anything in the present is identical to the actual origin event. All that is necessary is that one be able to find analogies in the present from which he can speculate about the past. For instance, one does not have to find life spontaneously generating from nonlife in the present in order to scientifically speculate on its purely natural origins. All that is necessary is to reconstruct similar situations where some telltale feature of life can be produced naturally. Likewise, a plausible creation scenario does not need an identical cause (e.g., the Creator) to produce life in the present. All that is necessary is to observe that like intelligent causes regularly produce some telltale feature of life. So a primary intelligent cause of the world or life need not be identical to human intelligence but only similar to it. Whether there is evidence for such a creator is the subject of the next chapter.

Summary and Conclusion

Historically, modern science developed in terms of what we have called operation science, where secondary causes were used to describe regular, recurrent events. Early scientists banished final causes from the investigations of operation science, and with them, efficient causes. The myth of objective, philosophically neutral science was spawned and spread largely because both theists and naturalists agreed that science, that is, operation science, should be restricted to a study of secondary causes, which are continuously acting causes. This scientific method presupposed regular, recurrent events in order for hypotheses to be tested. When a science of origin studies began, a modified method, consistent with the new object of inquiry, was used. At first it seemed only natural to explain the origin of the universe by relying on the principle of uniformity and the study of secondary causes. In essence this provided a way to "work back" from the present operation of the universe. No formal distinction between operation science and origin science was made generally in science. Although the distinction between cosmology and cosmogony was made in astronomy, that distinction was not made in other disciplines (e.g., geology/geogony, biology/biogony, anthropology/anthropogony).*

Without the distinction between operation science and origin science it was believed that there is just one category for science, which is simply broadened in scope to allow origin scenarios to be considered scientific. The objective distinction between regular and singular events and the different methods used in inquiry was masked and treated as though it is a superficial difference. In fact it is a major reason philosophers of science have been unable to agree on the proper place for origin questions and on a definition of science. Origin-science scenarios cannot be tested against regular events because the events in question are singular. Therefore strictly speaking origin-science scenarios cannot be falsified if they are false. These scenarios must be evaluated on the basis of plausibility. Plausibility is judged by whether a scenario satisfies the principles of causality and

*It is interesting that Ernst Haeckel developed a similar terminology, although he seems not to have recognized that the objective basis for the distinctions required different methodologies for investigating regular and singular events.

uniformity (analogy) and generally conforms with the accumulated circumstantial evidence in a noncontradictory way.

Secondary-cause origin scenarios, such as Darwin's theory of evolution, have been judged plausible by many. Most scientists adhere to the one-category-for-science view and therefore have not considered the possibility of primary causes having a place in science. Primary efficient causes (as well as final causes) have been generally dismissed; they were thought to have been banished in the seventeenth century. However, we must distinguish primary efficient cause (a sculptor, artist, engineer, creator) from Aristotle's final cause (purpose, end). To banish final causes and teleology from science leaves untouched the question of primary efficient cause in origin science. Primary efficient cause, it is agreed, has no place in operation science. However, as long as the one-category-for-science view persisted it was not recognized that primary causes can have a place in origin science. Denying primary cause a place in origin science has been assumed but not justified (see chap. 5). Actually, to posit a primary efficient cause is legitimate in origin science if it validly conforms to the principle of uniformity (analogy). The plausibility of primary-cause origin scenarios will be addressed in the next chapter.

7

A General Outline
of a Creationist View
# of Origins

Two Basic Views of Origin Science:
Secondary Cause and Primary Cause

The Background of the Two Views

The question of origins can be cast into either a naturalistic or a theistic framework of thought (see appendix 2). As we have already seen, the early scientists had a theistic or deistic perspective (see chap. 2). This viewpoint is called primary-cause theism or theistic creationism. These scientists did not seem to recognize in general the possibility of a naturalistic primary cause (a viewpoint that is called primary-cause naturalism or naturalistic creationism). The failure to make these distinctions has led to much confusion in discussing origins. Early creationists posited a theistic primary cause beyond the universe as the explanation of the origin of the universe and of all living things. But except for Benedict Spinoza and a few others, early scientists did not recognize the possibility of a naturalistic primary cause. Early creationists also believed that God operates the universe by natural laws (secondary causes).

Scientists, whether theists or naturalists, were successful in discovering the laws of operation science. Eventually secondary causes (operation science) were extended to singularities and took over the field of origins (see chaps. 3–5). The whole of nature was viewed as a continuous web of interlocking secondary causes extending back indefinitely, if not infinitely.

With the advent of the big bang theory and modern physics, a totally naturalistic viewpoint was delivered a severe blow. No longer is nature viewed as an eternal and closed continuum of interlocking and determined events. A discontinuity exists at the beginning of the universe, and within the universe there is probability, not absolute necessity, of events. In short, it is not a closed universe but an open universe. This has reopened the door for historic views of origins which were set aside and ignored for more than a century after Charles Darwin, but never really disproved.

The Nature of the Two Views

The evolutionary approach to origins, which may be either naturalistic or theistic, searches for secondary causes within the universe (see appendix 2). The creationist view posits a primary cause of origins which may be beyond the universe and thus supernatural. Any attempt to limit causes of origins to purely natural (secondary) causes is misdirected historically, philosophically, and scientifically. Historically, the early scientists (such as Kepler, Newton, and Boyle) posited a primary supernatural cause of origins. This view has subsequently been judged to be philosophical or religious by many because they do not recognize origin science as a separate domain from operation science (see chap. 1).

Philosophically, naturalism and theism are logically exhaustive categories. Either nature is "the whole show" or it is not. That is, either there is a creator beyond and distinct from the cosmos (theism) or there is not (naturalism). Since the time of Darwin many have yielded to the temptation to bracket naturalism with secondary causes and theism with primary causes. But in fact each of these historic philosophic categories has both primary- and secondary-cause views. However, since the eighteenth century Western naturalism has insisted on secondary causes. Although historically theism has never exclusively favored one view or the other, many theists have tended to explain origins in terms of primary causes. But Eastern naturalism (e.g., some forms of Buddhism and Hinduism) often posits a primary cause within the universe (Hoyle and Wickramasinghe 1981). And many Western theists embrace the idea of origin by secondary causes, so the popular dichotomy of secondary-cause science versus primary-cause religion breaks down on closer inspection. It is legitimate for both theist and naturalist to raise the question of whether there was a primary or secondary cause of the origin events. And scientifically there is no way to rule out the possibility of a super-natural cause of origins.

The Three Main Areas of Concern

This secondary-cause versus primary-cause approach to beginnings centers on three main areas: the origin of the universe, the origin of life, and the origin of new life forms (including human beings). The secondary-cause view in all three cases is generally called evolution, and the primary-cause view is generally called creation.* From the secondary-cause point of view these three areas are called cosmic evolution, biochemical evolution, and biological evolution. There are theists and naturalists who affirm this view. From the primary-cause point of view we could call these areas cosmic creation, biochemical creation, and biological creation. Philosophically, there are theists and naturalists who affirm this view. So it is important to note that calling oneself a creationist or evolutionist is not sufficient to determine whether one is speaking in the context of philosophical naturalism or theism. This is what makes the so-called creation-evolution debate so confusing. Actually, it is two debates. First it is a debate between theists and naturalists as to whether the cause is within or beyond the universe. Also it is a debate between primary- and secondary-causality views, with creationists favoring the former and evolutionists the latter.

Three Major Features of Origin-Science Investigations

A scientific approach to origins involves three major features: the principle of causality, the principle of uniformity (analogy), and circumstantial evidence. There are, of course, other characteristics of a good origins scenario, such as consistency and congruity with other related knowledge. But these being granted, the most significant issue is what kind of cause is plausibly posited for the origin event. In accordance with the principle of constant conjunction, plausibility

---

*Some evolutionists, however, admit to "creation" of the natural process and/or through it. And many creationists would admit to the use of some natural process in certain areas of creation. See appendix 2 for a full typology and treatment.

will be judged in terms of the ability to establish a repeatable conjunction of a certain kind of cause with a specific kind of effect. Thus one must evaluate plausibility in terms of the power of circumstantial evidence to establish a high probability of fact through inference.

The Principle of Causality

This principle, which states that "every event has a cause," has a venerable history in science. Even before the beginning of modern science, it was assumed that events have causes. Indeed, the origin of modern science was significantly influenced by the belief that God (a primary cause) had created the natural world. From the time of Francis Bacon onward it was recognized that the recurring events of nature, that is, the operation of nature, resulted from secondary causes. It is safe to say that without the belief in causes, whether primary or secondary, there would have been no science as we know it (see chaps. 2–4).

Basic to the principle of causality is the belief that things do not occur willy-nilly. If they did, science would not be possible. In fact, human life would be unlivable unless we could depend on regular causal conjunctions.

Contrary to a popular misunderstanding, Werner Heisenberg's principle of indeterminacy does not contradict the principle of causality. Heisenberg's principle is not the principle of uncausality but the principle of unpredictability. It is not that subatomic particle motion has no cause, but simply that scientists are unable to predict with accuracy where a specific particle will be at a given time. Even so, the overall probability pattern for all the particles in a system can be predicted under specified conditions. So there is not only causality of subatomic particle behavior, but also regularity and predictability of the pattern of distributed particles, even though the exact course of any individual particle is not known.

One possible cause which can be posited for events in the domain of origin science is a primary cause. Isaac Newton argued that only a primary cause is an adequate explanation for the order manifest in the heavens. William Paley immortalized the argument for a primary (intelligent) cause in his design argument (see appendix 1). However, without the benefit of a distinct domain of origin science those arguments by Newton and Paley are considered by many to be outside the bounds of science. Even if their arguments are considered valid they are still called philosophy or religion. Such has been the plight of creationist views ever since. Consideration of primary causes had been banished from the realm of science. However, as we saw in the previous chapter, recent trends in physics and astronomy have reopened the door for primary-cause explanations.

For creationists a primary cause is an intelligent cause and is often called a creator. It is called primary (first) because it is the ultimate source, the first mover of the effect in question. It is the who, not the how, by which the effect arose. In classical terminology a primary cause is an efficient cause. That is, it is the agent by which the effect is produced, as opposed to an instrumental cause (that through which), or a final cause (that for which) something is produced. A primary cause is a producing cause. It is the necessary and sufficient condition for the effect.

A secondary cause was so named because it was believed to be the means the Creator (first Cause) used in operating the universe. Secondary causes are natural causes. They describe how the world operates. They are used exclusively by those who hold evolutionary views. Darwin's principle of natural selection is an example. He believed that this principle replaced the need to posit a creator for the origin of new species. Darwin even called it "my deity 'Natural Selection'" (letter to Charles Lyell, Oct. 20, 1859; Darwin 1888).

Historically, modern scientists came increasingly to seek secondary causes to explain singular origin events (see chaps. 3–4). Their success in finding secondary (natural) causes for the regular operation of the universe was applied to the problem of accounting for the unique singular events of origin as well. This approach was based on the premise that nature is a continuum of secondary causes and effects. This, however, has become suspect with the acceptance of the big bang theory. Positing a radical discontinuity at the very beginning of the universe has served to reopen the door for entertaining the possibility of a primary cause for origins.

The question for a creationist view of origins is whether one can present evidence from the realm of origin science which supports positing a primary cause for the origin of the universe and of living things. This depends on the application of certain principles necessary for studying origin science.

The Principle of Uniformity (Analogy)

The most general way to state this principle is to say "the present is the key to the past." That is, the kind of cause that is observed to be regularly conjoined to a certain kind of effect in the present is assumed to have produced similar effects in the past. In short, similar effects have similar causes.

Since no two events are identical, no two causes need be identical. Thus the cause of past events need only be similar, not identical, to ones observed in the present. For example, makers of ancient pottery need not be exactly the same as current potters. Or, extraterrestrial intelligence (ETI) which might provide a message on a radio telescope (for SETI) need not be identical to human intelligence but only similar. Likewise, a creator (or primary-cause intelligence) posited to account for origin events may be similar to human intelligence, not identical.

In view of these two principles before us, the question for a creationist view of origin science is this: Is there scientific evidence, based on observation of regularly occurring causal conjunctions, which points to a primary cause of the universe, of first life, and/or of new life forms? It will not suffice for the creationist simply to point to the lack of evidence for a secondary cause of life. From no evidence no scientific conclusion follows. Some positive evidence for creation must be presented before a positive conclusion can be drawn.

Circumstantial Evidence

Sometimes no analogy is available in the present. In such cases it might still be possible to make a persuasive case on the basis of circumstantial evidence. This is like the approach of a lawyer in a capital case of murder. In lieu of eyewitness testimony a convincing case might still be developed by weaving together circumstantial evidence. As we shall see, in the question of the origin of the universe no valid analogy is available, but there is circumstantial evidence. Likewise, the fossil record is circumstantial evidence that both creationists and evolutionists use in support of their respective cases.

The Three Basic Areas of Origin Science

There are three major areas of concern for origin science: the origin of the universe, the origin of first life, and the origin of new life forms (including human beings). It is not our purpose here to present detailed evidence for a theistic creationist (primary-cause theist)*

*See appendix 2.

view of these areas but only to sketch an outline of the direction such a creationist view may take.

A Theistic Creationist View of the Origin of the Universe

The general logic of such a creationist origin-science view of the beginning of the universe is this:

1. Every event has a cause.
2. The universe had a beginning.
3. Therefore, the universe had a cause.

Since the first premise is a basic premise of science, we need not argue for its legitimacy here but simply note several things about it.

First, it begs the question in favor of philosophical naturalism to rule out in advance the possibility of positing a supernatural cause for the origin of the universe, especially if there is evidence the universe had a beginning. Indeed, the scientific method as such should not be committed to either philosophical naturalism or supernaturalism (theism).

Second, if as a matter of fact the whole physical universe (i.e., nature) came into existence, then a nonnatural (i.e., supernatural) cause is not only possible, but also plausible. The only theoretical alternative is a mathematical possibility arising from some of Albert Einstein's equations, which seems on its face to be a form of semantic mysticism, that is, "nothingness pregnant with being" (Weizsacker 1964, 36). A more sophisticated expression of the same view comes from what is called the new cosmology. It amounts to literal creation ex nihilo, by natural laws. The significance of this view for naturalistic minds is stated well by Paul Davies:

> This new physics and the new cosmology hold out a tantalizing prom-
> ise: that we *might* be able to explain how all the physical structures in
> the universe have come to exist, automatically, as a result of natural
> processes. We should *then* no longer have need for a creator in the
> traditional sense. (1984, 243, emphasis added)

Advocates of the new cosmology see their concept of a naturalistic ex nihilo beginning as displacing at last the supernatural Creator. As Davies expressed it, "We can at last comprehend a universe free of all supernatural input, a universe that is completely the product of natural laws accessible to science" (ibid., 10).*

Davies is here thinking in terms of operation science, where it is indeed appropriate to attempt to displace false views with better secondary-cause natural hypotheses. But in origin science the events in question are unique (a class of one) and hypotheses about how they occurred cannot be empirically falsified. The proper goal of origin science is to offer a plausible origins view, where plausibility is established on the basis of either a legitimate analogy or convincing circumstantial evidence or both.

Third, raising questions as to whether a theistic primary cause of the universe had a cause, ad infinitum, is fruitless. To insist that an uncaused first Cause beyond the universe explains nothing is to forget that likewise an uncaused first effect or superforce would explain nothing either. Both the naturalist and the theist posit something which is uncaused. The naturalist claims it is the universe or some naturalistic superforce, while the theist holds that it is a supernatural Creator of the cosmos.

Finally, some have suggested infinite regress of causes. But this is based on the false premise that "everything has a cause," which is not what the principle of causality claims. It does not hold that "every*thing* has a cause" but only that "every *event* has a cause." Since beginning or coming to be is an event, then whatever began had a cause. But what does not begin or come to be does not need a cause, whether it is a creator or the universe.

In view of the principle of causality, the basic question for the creationist is this: Is there empirical evidence that the universe (cosmos) had a beginning? If there is, then it is reasonable to posit a primary cause (creator) of the universe. The alternative is to throw off the collective perception of the whole Western world that all events have a cause, and assert that superevents of origin have no cause. However plausible this may seem to a complete naturalist, it will seem to the primary-cause theist to be a case of special pleading. For surely there is nothing implausible about positing a supernatural cause for the superevent of the creation of the natural universe.

*Paul Davies's hypothesis has been effectively countered by William L. Craig. He shows that there is no scientific basis for claiming that nothing produces something. For "all that actually occurs [on the subatomic level] is conversion of energy into matter or vice versa." (William L. Craig, "God, Creation and Mr. Davies," *British Journal of Philosophy of Science* 37 [1986]: 165).

The scientific case for the beginning of the universe

Contemporary astronomy has provided several lines of evidence for a beginning of the natural universe. Robert Jastrow summarized it well when he wrote, "Now three lines of evidence—the motions of the galaxies, the laws of thermodynamics, and the life story of the stars—pointed to one conclusion: all indicated that the Universe had a beginning" (1978, 111). Actually we have here observational and circumstantial evidences giving an argument within the domain of origin science. The origin events in question are clearly singular and thus form no part of operation science.

The laws of thermodynamics. The first law of thermodynamics is the law of energy conservation. It states that the amount of actual energy in the universe remains constant. No energy* is being created or destroyed. There is a fixed amount of total energy in the universe. But the second law of thermodynamics is the law of entropy. It states that in a closed isolated system, such as the whole universe, the amount of usable energy is decreasing. Things are tending to disorder; the universe is running down.

But if the universe is running out of usable energy, then it is not infinite (since it cannot run out of an infinite amount of usable energy). Thus the second law of thermodynamics strongly suggests that the material universe (cosmos) had a beginning.

The universe is expanding. Another evidence that the universe is not eternal is the inference that it is expanding, as if from an initial point of beginning. This is based on the observation that the stars are moving farther apart from each other. Recent advances in astronomy appear to have confirmed this.

> The most complete study made thus far has been carried out on the 200-inch telescope by Allan Sandage. He compiled information on 42 galaxies, ranging out in space as far as six billion light years from us. His measurements indicate that the Universe was expanding more rapidly in the past than it is today. This result lends further support to the belief that the Universe exploded into being. (Ibid., 95)

The radiation "echo." Another independent line of evidence that the universe exploded into being and is thus of finite age is the discovery of a universal radiation "echo." Jastrow notes,

---

*Actually by Einstein's famous equation $E = mc^2$, energy and mass form a total that is conserved.

No explanation other than the big bang has been found for the fireball radiation. The clincher, which has convinced almost the last doubting Thomas, is that the radiation discovered by Penzias and Wilson has exactly the pattern of wavelengths expected for the light and heat produced in a great explosion. Supporters of the Steady State theory have tried desperately to find an alternative explanation, but they have failed. (Ibid., 5)

Thus there are three lines of scientific evidence which are offered to support the theory that the universe had a beginning. Combined these arguments make a compelling case from modern science that the universe had a beginning. Despite his confessed agnosticism, Jastrow acknowledges that "the scientist's pursuit of the past ends in the moment of creation . . . . Science has proved that the Universe exploded into being at a certain moment" (ibid., 114–15). Or as Davies put it, "The most important scientific discovery of our age is that the physical universe did not always exist" (1984, 5).

In the light of this evidence Jastrow concludes,

Now we see how the astronomical evidence leads to a biblical view of the origin of the world. The details differ, but the essential elements in the astronomical and biblical accounts of Genesis are the same: the chain of events leading to man commenced suddenly and sharply at a definite moment in time, in a flash of light and energy. (1978, 14)

The case for a supernatural cause of the universe

Since Jastrow understands science in terms of operation science, it is understandable that he hesitates as a scientist to conclude there was a primary cause of the universe. He leaves this to faith, simply noting that "there are limits to the power of scientific inquiry" (1982, 16). However, it is interesting to note that by using only the principles of operation science, those working in a strictly Western naturalistic tradition have had to admit the mounting evidence for a beginning of the universe.

With science limited to one domain (operation science), Jastrow sees no way to get behind the origin event. "All this happened as a product of forces |scientists| cannot hope to discover." That is, by using secondary-cause methods he can get back to the origin but cannot tell what caused it. Thus he asserts agnosticism. But origin science allows the possibility of a primary cause of the origin of the universe (see chap. 6). And since such a cause would be beyond the natural universe, this primary cause would be supernatural. Jastrow implied as much when he said, "That there are what I or anyone would call supernatural forces at work is now, I think, a scientifically proven fact" (ibid., 15, 18). These are strong words for an avowed agnostic, and they fit well into a creationist origin-science view of the origin of the universe by a first cause. However, what Jastrow probably meant is that the cause is beyond our present concept of secondary cause. This is because he sees only one domain for science, that of operation science. Thus he believes that any further comment must come by faith, from beyond science. However, with the recognition of the category of origin science, one is able to posit a supernatural cause for the origin of the universe.

Does this mean that one can prove by origin science that a creator exists? No, not in any strict sense of the term *proof*. For it is always possible that the big bang is only the most recent explosion in a long (or endless) series of explosions. It is also possible, as the steady state theory proposes, that hydrogen atoms are spontaneously appearing in the universe to keep things from running down. It is possible that the universe simply came into being "from nothing and by nothing," as some atheists claim. However, there is a tremendous price one must pay to embrace this strange conclusion; one must sacrifice one of the great foundation stones of modern science, the conviction that every event has a cause. Not even the skeptic David Hume would accept "so absurd a proposition as that anything might arise without a cause" (1932, 1:187). Yet the new cosmologists are doing just that. Their basis is certain alleged theoretical possibilities they believe arise out of quantum physics. As Davies sees it, and quite a few agree, "quantum physics offers the only branch of science in which the concept of an event without a cause makes sense" (1984, 203).

This, however, is a misunderstanding (see Craig 1986, 163–75). Quantum physics simply makes the causal connections probabilistic rather than deterministic. It seems a long shot to throw off the accumulated experience of Western science. At any rate it is an insufficient basis to counter the plausibility, within origin science, of a supernatural creator.

A Theistic Creationist View of the Origin of First Life*

It has long been recognized by those on both sides of the issue that there are only two basic views on the origin of first life. As Jastrow

*This section is dependent on the excellent book of Charles B. Thaxton, Walter L. Bradley, and Roger L. Olsen, *The Mystery of Life's Origin* (1984).

noted, "Either life was created on the earth by the will of a being outside the grasp of scientific understanding, or it evolved on our planet spontaneously, through chemical reactions occurring in non-living matter lying on the surface of the planet" (1977, 62). Of course, life could have begun on another planet, but then there were only two alternatives there: secondary-cause chemical evolution (spontaneous generation) or primary-cause creation. As Nobel Prize-winning biologist George Wald expressed it, "There is no third position" ([1954] 1979, 38).

Creationists have sometimes been content to point to the lack of evidence for a secondary-cause evolutionary explanation of the origin of life. But this approach is unsuccessful for several reasons. First, the lack of evidence for one secondary-cause view does not automatically indicate the need for a primary-cause view. Why not some other secondary-cause view? Second, for those who operate in a one-category science, a primary cause is not a viable option. As J. W. N. Sullivan wrote,

> It became an accepted doctrine that life never arises except from life. So far as actual evidence goes, this is still the only possible conclusion. But since it is a conclusion that seems to lead back to some super-natural creative act, it is a conclusion that scientific men find very difficult of acceptance. [1933, 94]

But this complete rejection of the supernatural is no longer tenable in view of the recognition that the universe had a beginning. It manifests an unacceptable naturalistic bias in the area of origin science which is at odds with the strong evidence for a radical discontinuity at the beginning of the universe. If there could plausibly be a supernatural primary cause at the beginning of the cosmos, then there could also be a primary cause (possibly supernatural) for the origin of life. In the domain of origin science such a view and its supporting evidence may be presented.

There is mounting evidence that the origin of life has not been plausibly accounted for by purely secondary causes. First, there is no evidence for the "prebiotic soup," as is proposed in nearly all the chemical-evolution theories. Second, the chemical-soup hypothesis does not take into account the many destructive forces at work (Thaxton, Bradley, and Olsen 1984, chap. 4). Third, the experiments by Stanley Miller and Harold C. Urey, for example, involve illegitimate investigator interference—which if anything supports a creationist view of intelligent intervention (see ibid., chap. 6). Fourth, there is the serious problem of how to convert energy flow through the system into information.

In response to the strong case against the secondary-cause chemical-evolution view some novel solutions have been posited. They include the suggestion that new laws need to be discovered, and others that hold life was formed naturally elsewhere in the cosmos and then found its way here on a comet, or perhaps on an alien spaceship. Still other views suggest novel habitats on earth where life might have had a natural origin. Some have looked in the vicinity of sea-floor thermal vents, or have considered that life might originally have formed on clay minerals. This latter possibility is currently attracting the attention of NASA scientists and others who see a way to avoid most of the objections raised against the chemical-soup hypothesis.

Some of these scenarios have been shown to be more plausible than the chemical-soup hypothesis. But the same fundamental problem remains, namely, how to account for the specific sequences of biochemical "letters" in the formation of biological information. Such information is thought to be responsible for biological function. So any satisfactory account of the origin of life must plausibly explain biological information.

Interestingly it is this most difficult problem for all secondary-cause scenarios to date that most readily and quite plausibly can be accounted for by positing a primary (intelligent) cause. The positive evidence for an intelligent primary cause of the origin of life is strong. For purposes of the argument for a primary cause of the origin of life, it is not necessary to know what is meant by life. It is necessary only to identify some distinguishing feature of life. Leslie Orgel summarizes the essential distinctions in these words: "Living organisms are distinguished by their *specified complexity*. Crystals . . . fail to qualify as living because they lack *complexity*; random mixtures of polymers fail to qualify because they lack *specificity*" (1973, 189, emphasis added).

The similarity between the specified complexity of life's informational polymers and the specificity of letters in a written language is striking. In fact, as information scientist Hubert P. Yockey has pointed out, they are "mathematically identical" (1981, 16). Three sets of letter arrangements will illustrate the differences between order, unspecified complexity, and specified complexity:

Letter Arrangements

1. Orderly (periodic) and therefore specified
   GIFT   GIFT   GIFT   GIFT
   Example: crystal, nylon

2. Complex (aperiodic) and unspecified
   TGELSIDHT   TBWORMHQC   PUQXHDMBT
   Example: random polymer (polypeptides)

3. Complex (aperiodic) and specified
   A message is riding on this sequence
   Example: protein

The set of symbols GIFT is used to illustrate that meaning is extraneous to the sequence, arbitrary, and depends on some symbol convention. The word *gift*, which in English means "present," and in German "poison," in French is meaningless. This is not to suggest that there is even this much information in a crystal or regular polymer like nylon. The illustration shows, however, that even if there were, it would be drowned in a sea of redundancy. This lack of variability in a crystal means that all code potential is effaced (see Thaxton, Bradley, and Olsen 1984, 129–30).

The greatest evidence in support of a primary-cause creation view comes from the analogy that has been used to support creation from time immemorial. For constant observation reveals that only intelligence is the known cause of the complex information found in pottery, sculpture, art, books, machines, and now, genes and proteins.* This, of course, is the famous design argument which, due to recent advances in the study of molecules, can be sharply focused and applied to the origin of life (see appendix 1).

Boundary conditions and specified complexity

There are several factors to consider in a primary-cause scenario of origins. The first is the nature of what is known as specified complexity, which involves the imposing of boundary conditions.

---

*The genes and proteins referred to here are those synthesized in chemical laboratories through the informative intervention of the investigators.

In a most illuminating article entitled "Life's Irreducible Structure," Michael Polanyi pointed out that a host of uniquely human activities, whether of making a sculpture, composing a painting, playing chess, writing a book, building a machine, or synthesizing insulin in a laboratory, is characterized by the "imposing of *boundary conditions* on the laws of physics and chemistry." A boundary condition is a restriction on the working of nature, "a set of conditions that is explicitly left undetermined by the laws of nature" (Polanyi 1968, 1308, emphasis added).

The point Polanyi makes about boundary conditions is worth elaborating. Sometimes the boundary condition restricts or limits nature in order that an experimenter may observe nature's behavior under these altered conditions. But it is nature that is still the focus of the investigation. At other times an investigator may be interested in the boundary conditions per se and nature or the materials involved are irrelevant to the investigation. Polanyi illustrates:

> When a saucepan bounds a soup that we are cooking, we are interested in the soup; and, likewise, when we observe a reaction in a test tube, we are studying the reaction, not the test tube. The reverse is true for a game of chess. The strategy of the player imposes boundaries on the several moves which follow the laws of chess, but our interest lies in the boundaries—that is, in the strategy, not in the several moves as exemplification of the laws. And similarly, when a sculptor shapes a stone or a painter composes a painting, our interest lies in the boundaries imposed on a material, and not in the material itself. (Ibid., 1308)

Consider the effects of a skywriter, a person who imposes a boundary on smoke by intelligently controlling the release of smoke from an airplane. No physical boundary has been imposed, but a boundary of thought. In other words, the material itself does not form its own boundaries. They are imposed on the material by an intelligent agent. A boundary of thought was also imposed on the stone of Mount Rushmore in order to form the faces of the presidents there. Likewise, a boundary of thought was imposed on the sand of the beach when John wrote, "John loves Mary."

In these three illustrations the focus is also on the boundary conditions which fundamentally "transcend the laws of physics and chemistry," as Polanyi said (1967a, 54), and not on the medium or material used. In each case the boundary condition had its origin in intelligent thought and was then imposed on inert material, whether it was smoke, stone, or sand.

The discussion about boundary conditions dovetails into the point about specified complexity. The term *boundary condition* is taken from physics where it has a specific meaning and a long history of use. The term *specified complexity* is more recent; it was coined in the attempt to describe living organisms in a way that distinguished them from structures that are specified but not complex (such as a crystal) or structures that are complex but not specified (such as a random mixture of polymers). As Orgel said, "The crystals fail to qualify as living because they lack complexity; the mixture of polymers fail to qualify because they lack specificity" (1973, 189).

Two points arise out of the discussion about boundary conditions and specified complexity. First, in a communication system like a book, the boundary condition itself is what is of interest. In other words, the communication is the boundary condition, and the communication is independent of the medium by which it is conveyed. The communication is the same whether it is written on paper, stone, sand, or with smoke released from a plane. The medium, however, does affect the degree of permanency. The second point arising from the discussion is that specified complexity and communication-type boundary conditions are known experientially to arise by the intelligent shaping of matter, that is, by a primary efficient cause.

Specified complexity in DNA

A development in the study of DNA adds another piece of evidence to the primary-cause scenario of origins. It has been recognized for many years that the genetic communication system works like a book. That is, the communication is carried along in the exact sequence of letters, irrespective of whether the alphabet is twenty-six English letters, twenty-four letters of Greek, or the four letters of the genetic alphabet. This is called the sequence hypothesis. In a detailed analysis of the subject of specificity (i.e., specified complexity) in DNA and in written language, Yockey notes, "It is important to understand that we are not reasoning by analogy. The sequence hypothesis applies directly to the protein and the genetic text as well as to written language and therefore the treatment is mathematically identical." Thus it can be assumed that whenever one observes sequences manifesting such specified complexity that a primary intelligent cause is called for. When chance is invoked to explain such complex information, it becomes the "God-of-the-gaps" of naturalism.

The primary-cause scenario and the principle of uniformity

Throughout this book we have maintained that where possible a valid origin-science view is strongest if it conforms to the principle of uniformity, that is, analogy. That is, when observation in the present establishes a constant conjunction between a certain kind of cause and a certain kind of effect, then we can plausibly posit that kind of cause for that kind of effect in the past. It is now time to draw together converging lines of evidence in the argument to show that the primary-cause scenario of the creation of life does in fact satisfy the demands of a legitimate origin science.

First of all, there is evidence that a primary cause of specified complexity does exist in the present. Books, statues, bridges, machines, and art are an enduring testimony that intelligent shaping of matter (by a primary efficient cause) does regularly produce specified complexity. On the basis of the principle of uniformity it can be concluded that similar ancient artifacts also were produced by a primary cause. The science of archaeology is based on this logic. The question is raised as to whether it is valid to use this reasoning to infer a primary efficient cause in the past before man. But the conclusion must rest on the evidence, as all good science maintains, not on a priori assumptions. And there is empirical testimony to the existence of specified complexity before man. For the simplest form of life with its store of DNA is characterized by specified complexity. Yet such life is widely acknowledged to have existed before human life appeared.

The mathematical identity of the specified complexity of DNA and of a written language is a telling piece of evidence. Specified complexity is the hallmark of intelligent (primary efficient cause) activity. This approach is routinely used by NASA teams to evaluate data from planets and their moons in the search for intelligent life. For example, if macrolevel structures such as the famed Martian "canals" were documented it would confirm the presence of intelligent life there.

Astronomy provides another example where contemporary scientists assume an intelligent primary cause of certain kinds of events. The search for extraterrestrial intelligence (SETI) has raised the question as to how one would recognize a signal received on a radio telescope. The well-known astronomer Carl Sagan believes that even a single message from outer space would establish the existence of ETI. He wrote:

> There are others who believe that our problems are soluble, that humanity is still in its childhood, that one day soon we will grow up. The receipt of *a single message from space* would show that it is possible to live through such technological adolescence: the transmitting civilization, after all, has survived. Such knowledge, it seems to me, might be worth a great price. (1979, 275, emphasis added)

NASA recently constructed a thousand-foot radio telescope in Arecibo, Puerto Rico, where it will scan 773 stars within eighty light years in hope of hearing a message from ETI. This project is called SETI (search for extraterrestrial intelligence). *Time* magazine adds, "Astronomers have little trouble imagining the form such a simple message might take; one giving certain basic facts about life on Earth was actually trasmitted from Arecibo, aimed at a globular cluster of stars some 25,000 light-years away, for three minutes one day back in 1974" (Jan. 31, 1983, 64). The optimism of some scientists connected with the SETI program is high. One said, "This decade may be the first time in history to provide clear evidence of intelligent life elsewhere" (McDonough 1983, 3).

Even if the message is not decodeable, nevertheless it can be easily recognized that it has an intelligent source. For one can distinguish the difference between static on a radio (caused by sunspot activity) and a message in Morse code, or some other code, even if one does not know the code. One of the marvels of modern communications engineering is its ability to pull out a discernible message from the hiss of radio noise. This is possible because an intelligent message manifests specified complexity.

According to the principle of uniformity, if effects from the past and the present are shown to be the same kind, and the cause of the present effects is known or repeatedly observed, then it is plausible to assign the same kind of cause to the effect in the past. We conclude therefore that since DNA and written language both exhibit the property of specified complexity, and since intelligence (primary cause) is known to produce written communication, it is plausible to posit a primary cause as the source of DNA in the past.

Some have sought to blunt the force of this argument by saying that the primary cause of specified complexity in machines, books, or art is itself the product of the secondary cause of natural selection (Orgel 1973, 196–97). This response is entirely inadequate. It begs the fundamental question, namely, what is the source of the specified complexity in DNA? Since it is generally regarded that natural selection presupposes replicating systems in order to operate, we agree with noted evolutionist Theodosius Dobzhansky that "prebiotic natural selection is a contradiction in terms" (1965, 310). In the prebiotic world there were no living, evolving organisms to select. Indeed, the analogy between the specified complexity of DNA in living cells and other complex information, such as that in books, is so great that it is found to be "mathematically identical."

In view of this strong analogy between complex information in a written language and in living things, it seems that Paley has been misread by many moderns. For it was this same kind of argument which Paley used in his famous watchmaker argument. Using Hume's very phrase *uniform experience*, Paley insisted that

> wherever we see marks of contrivance, we are led for its cause to an *intelligent* author. And this transition of the understanding is founded upon *uniform experience*. We see intelligence constantly contriving; that is, we see intelligence constantly producing effects, marked and distinguished by certain properties—not certain particular properties, but by a kind and class of properties, such as relation to an end, relation of parts to one another and to a common purpose. We see, wherever we are witnesses to the actual formation of things, nothing except intelligence producing effects so marked and distinguished in the same manner. We wish to account for their origin. Our experience suggests a cause perfectly adequate to this account. No experience, no single instance or example, can be offered in favor of any other. ([1802] 1963, 37, emphasis added)

So Paley is not refuted by Hume (in advance), as many believe. Rather he actually builds his argument for an intelligent cause on Hume's principle of uniformity or constant conjunction. That is, Paley's watchmaker argument is not effectively countered by noting that one can validly conclude a watchmaker made a watch only if he has previously observed the like of watches being made by watchmakers. For it is precisely Paley's point that uniform previous experience informs us that the like of the complex order found in living things is produced regularly by an intelligent being. And lacking knowledge of molecular biology and DNA, Paley had no idea just how complex the information in a "simple" living cell really is. In short, thanks to molecular biology Paley's design argument is even stronger today than when he formulated it (see appendix 1).

If Paley's argument for an intelligent creator of life is so strong, why have so many modern thinkers rejected it? There seem to be several reasons for this situation.

First, following Hume's argument against miracles there was a confusion of the basis and object of scientific enquiry (see chap. 5). Hume had correctly argued that the *basis* for knowledge about past events is regularity or uniformity (constant conjunction). But this in no way precludes the *object* from being a singularity. If it does then the singularities of big bang, of the spontaneous origin of life, and the singular transitions in the evolution of life that most scientists accept would also be unscientific. But granting that there are authentic singularities in the past, which are understood (or inferred) in terms of present regularities, then there is no reason one cannot posit an intelligent creator of the first living thing. And since the plausibility of the primary cause being supernatural has already been established, by way of the big bang theory of origin, there is no reason to assume the primary cause of first life could not be supernatural as well.

Second, another reason Paley has been wrongly dismissed is the failure of many to see the legitimate difference between origin science (to which Paley's type of argument can be applied) and operation science. The tendency to think in one-category science has been dominant since the early nineteenth century (see chaps. 3–4). Once operation science, which seeks only secondary causes, was developed, it tended to dominate the area once held for origins, which admitted primary causation. But in origin science, now that the big bang theory and quantum physics have reopened the door to consider singularities, there is no reason the design argument for created singularities should be summarily dismissed.

Third, since Hume and particularly Laplace, the design argument has been wrongly sidetracked into the direction of probability rather than being based on an observed constant conjunction or regularity. Some have argued, for example, that even though the odds against life forming by pure chance are admittedly slim, nonetheless given enough time it could happen (Wald [1954] 1979).* Indeed, even though the chances for rolling three sixes are 1/216, yet one some-

*Wald has more recently acknowledged that time alone is not sufficient for this task.

times gets it on the first roll. Philosophic naturalists argue that the origin of the universe and life could likewise be a "lucky roll."

Putting it this way would effectively counter Paley's argument, but it is also contrary to the essential *basis* of science, namely, *constant conjunction*. For the question is not what are the theoretical possibilities about the past but what are the actual regularities of the present in terms of which one can understand the past. Scientific understanding is not based on luck or odd events. Rather, it is grounded in repeated experience of constant conjunction. And there is a constant conjunction between an intelligent cause and the kind of complex information found in a living cell. Hence, a primary-cause explanation of the origin of life is plausible because it is based on more than theoretical possibility; it is based on observable uniformity or constant conjunction.

Fourth, another reason Paley has been rejected by modern scientists is his emphasis on teleology or purpose in nature. Since the time of Darwin natural selection has been widely accepted as an explanation of much of the so-called purpose in nature (see Moore 1979, 280–311). This being the case, Paley's argument has been weakened. However, even if one sets aside the question of teleology (final cause), this in no way eliminates the need for an efficient cause. Origin science as such need not be concerned with the purpose of creation. It can focus on the need for an intelligent producer without thereby being entangled in the question of what purpose was in mind. For one can reasonably posit an intelligent cause for the portrait of Mona Lisa without knowing what purpose Leonardo da Vinci had in painting it.

A Theistic Creationist View of the Origin of New Life Forms

Prior to Darwin the official scientific view of origins was creation. Darwin even referred to it as "the theory of creation" ([1859] 1958, 235). It was not from the beginning perceived as unscientific, as is the opinion of most scientists today. This is due primarily to the failure to distinguish origin science as a separate domain from operation science (see chap. 6).

The conclusion here is that origin science is the proper domain for carrying out the scientific investigation of origins, whether creation or evolution. Only in origin science can it be shown in what sense creation and evolution are both legitimate candidates for any type of scientific consideration.

In origin science the plausibility of a hypothesis is established through a valid analogy between present and past, or through circumstantial evidence. The greatest plausibility, of course, will attend a view if both valid analogy and convincing circumstantial evidence are offered. This is the approach Darwin took in his *Origin of Species*. He presented both analogy and circumstantial evidence which he artfully combined in "one long argument" to effectively persuade his reader.

Michael Ruse (1982, 44–45) has argued that Darwin used both analogy and circumstantial evidence in the *Origin* to satisfy the leading theorists of the day on proper scientific method. John Herschel was a famous astronomer who had written popular books on the proper method of conducting scientific inquiry. Herschel's method emphasized analogy, which is a convincing inferential tool. If an analogy to a known cause could be presented, a view was regarded as scientific.

On the other hand, William Whewell, who coined the word *scientist* in 1840, was also a popular writer about science. His approach was inductive, espousing circumstantial evidence as the mark of good science. So what Darwin did, according to Ruse, was to use both approaches in the *Origin*.

Darwin based the analogy part of his argument on artificial selection. Darwin himself was a pigeon breeder, and many others of the time were actively breeding sheep, dogs, or cattle. Breeding experiments had demonstrated only limited change, and biologists were dismissing any suggestions that domestication might be analogous to nature. Alfred Wallace, who independently developed ideas on natural selection, argued quite vehemently that artificial selection is irrelevant to the question of evolution. Critics said there was no true analogy since nature is blind and unintelligent, quite unlike the breeders. E. S. Russell wrote:

It is unfortunate that Darwin ever introduced the term "natural selection", for it has given rise to much confusion of thought. He did so, of course, because he arrived at his theory through studying the effects of selection as practised by man in the breeding of domesticated animals and cultivated plants. Here the use of the word is entirely legitimate. But the *action of man in selective breeding is not analogous to the action of "natural selection", but almost its direct opposite*. . . . Man has an aim or an end in view; "natural selection" can have none. Man picks out the individuals he wishes to cross, choosing them by the characters he seeks to perpetuate or enhance. He protects them and their issue by all means in his power, guarding them thus from the operation of natural selection, which would speedily eliminate many freaks; he continues his active and purposeful selection from generation to generation until he reaches, if possible, his goal. Nothing of this kind happens, or can happen, through the blind process of differential elimination and differential survival which we miscall "natural selection". ([1915] 1962, 124; cited in Moore 1979)

This insightful critique can be summarized as it is in table 1.

TABLE 1

Natural Selection and Macroevolution

Evolutionary thesis: If artificial selection can produce significant changes in a short time, then natural selection can make even greater changes over long periods of time.

	The Crucial Differences	
	Artificial selection	Natural selection
Goal	Aim (end) in view	No aim (end) in view
Process	Intelligently guided process	Blind process
Choices	Intelligent choice of breeds	No intelligent choice of breeds
Protection	Breeds guarded from destructive processes	Breeds not guarded from destructive processes
Freaks	Preserves desired freaks	Eliminates most freaks
Interruptions	Continued interruptions to reach desired goal	No continued interruptions to reach any goal
Survival	Preferential survival	Nonpreferential survival

Conclusion: Rather than being similar, artificial selection and natural selection are in most crucial respects exactly opposite. Thus the analogy is invalid.

This criticism, which was not unknown to Darwin, makes it all the more remarkable that he drew an analogy between artificial selection and natural selection. In the words of Ruse, the analogy is not only used, "it is flaunted" (1982, 48). Even though Darwin recognized the evidence for a link between artificial and natural selection is weak, he quite simply needed the analogy to satisfy the demands of theorists like Herschel (ibid., 48).

The lack of a true analogy did not deter Darwin. After all, the process he envisioned would take many generations before the slightest change might be detected. So despite lack of observational evidence Darwin felt justified in using Natural Selection, personifying it and ascribing to it the breeder-like power to "pick out with unerring skill the best varieties." He thought blind and unguided nature could do in hundreds or thousands of generations what breeders could do in a few.

To reinforce the idea of origins by natural selection Darwin cited an enormous amount of circumstantial evidence,* including the great "testimony" of the fossils. Fossils are the only hard evidence available. So it is a vital question to ask, What is contained in the fossil record? Following the advice to "go and see," we discover a succession of fossil appearances in the record, starting with invertebrates on the bottom. Above them are fishes, then amphibia. Higher still are reptiles, then birds, and finally mammals, eventually coming to man. Surely this fact of the fossils is significant, and it provided circumstantial evidence for a progression of creatures through their history.

This sequential appearance of fossils in the record is shown in nearly every introductory biology book. This evidence was used by Darwin to support the analogy based on artificial selection. He believed fossil evidence would support his contention of gradual transitions between major categories of life forms. It seemed to follow from his understanding of the slow but gradual working of natural selection. But the fossil record confronted Darwin with a major problem too. In *The Origin of Species* he asks rhetorically, "Why then is not every geological formation and every stratum full of such intermediate links? Geology assuredly does not reveal any such finely graduated organic chain, and this, perhaps, is the most obvious and gravest objection which can be urged against my theory" ([1859] 1958, 280).

In the 130 years since Darwin wrote the *Origin* much new paleontological evidence has come to light. Most of it has tended to accentuate this problem first noted by Darwin himself. The Harvard paleontologist Stephen Jay Gould says, "The extreme rarity of transitional forms in the fossil record persists as the trade secret of paleon-

---

*Additional circumstantial evidence was used, which today has grown to include comparative anatomy, embryology, comparative biochemistry, and chromosome structure. However, our purpose is merely to show the basic form of origin science, not to give a survey of the circumstantial evidence.

tology. The evolutionary trees that adorn our textbooks have data only at the tips and nodes of their branches; the rest is inference, however reasonable, not the evidence of fossils" (1977, 14).

As a result of the gaps in the fossil record a revolution is currently going on within evolutionary ranks. On the one side are the traditionalists who, in spite of the gaps, persist in their view of gradual evolution through small slow changes. On the other side are the punctuationalists, those who repudiate gradualism and state that evolution occurred at a more erratic or jerky pace in which species appear "suddenly" in a few tens of thousands of years.

The new view is just as committed to secondary-cause evolution as the traditional view. The essential difference between them is the proposal that calmness characterized perhaps 99 percent of evolutionary history, which was only occasionally punctuated by a sudden burst of speciation.

So far the punctuationalists lack a satisfactory mechanism to make plausible their view of "sudden" evolution. This makes them vulnerable to the criticism they are holding to a theory based on the mere absence of information, that is, missing fossils forming gaps in the record. After all, Darwin took suddenness as a sign of creation.

Although critics have picked away at various facets of Darwinian theory and the more modern evolutionary theories, few mainstream scientists have considered creationism a viable alternative. For most scientists this would entail not a major paradigm shift, but a total abandonment of science. Without benefit of the conceptual framework of origin science as a separate domain for considering origins hypotheses, including both creation and evolution, scientists have had little recourse but to place primary-cause creation outside the realm of legitimate science. As a result most scientists view organized efforts to promote creation science as simply misguided.

However, as we have seen, within origin science primary-cause creation is permissible, and will be deemed plausible if it meets the criteria of providing a valid analogy for its proposed cause, and/or can provide persuasive circumstantial evidence.

As in the case for evolution the fossil record is used as circumstantial evidence in support of creation.* Instead of the succession of

---

*See Wendell Bird, Brief of the State [of Louisiana] in Opposition to ACLU Motion for Summary Judgment (appendix 6) for a listing of creationist "affirmative evidence." Again, as in the earlier discussion of secondary causes, we are interested only in showing the form of origin science, not in detailing the circumstantial evidence.

fossil appearances emphasized by proponents of evolution and which creationists have had only partial success at explaining, creationists emphasize another feature of the fossils, which is just as characteristic and just as difficult for evolutionists to explain. When fossils first suddenly appear in the record they are fully formed and functional. No fossils of partial creatures appear in the record. And they remain unchanged through many strata and then suddenly disappear from the record. Many primary-cause creationists have emphasized this unmistakable feature of the fossil record (Gish 1973; Hoyle and Wickramasinghe 1981; Anderson and Coffin 1977). Louis Agassiz, the famous Harvard paleontologist, wrote,

> Species *appear suddenly* and disappear suddenly in progressive strata. That is the fact proclaimed by Palaeontology. . . . The geological record, even with all its imperfections, exaggerated to distortion, tells now, what it has told from the beginning, that the *supposed intermediate forms* between the species of different geological periods are *imaginary* beings, called up merely in support of a fanciful theory. (1860, 144–45)

This sudden appearance of fossils and their persistence without change (stasis) through many strata before their sudden disappearance was very widely held during Darwin's time to support creation. As Neal Gillespie has noted,

> All these men [Cuvier, Owen, Agassiz, Barrande, Falconer, Forbes, Lyell, Murchison, and Sedgwick] were paleontologists or geologists, and special *creation* . . . was commonly recognized by them to have *strong empirical evidence in the fossil series* which seemed to support the idea that species appeared full-blown suddenly, endured unchanged, and became extinct without leaving descendants. (1979, 26, emphasis added)

Such features of the fossil record were prima facie evidence of "full-blown" creation and were quite evidently an aggravation to Darwinians who were committed to the idea of gradual but constant change. For many years evolutionists were quiet about this most troubling feature of the fossil record. But punctuationalists now use this long-held creationist argument in favor of a new view. Gould claims that

> the history of most fossil species includes two features particularly inconsistent with gradualism:

1. *Stasis*. Most species exhibit no directional change during their tenure on earth. They appear in the fossil record looking much the same as when they disappear; morphological change is usually limited and directionless.
2. *Sudden appearance*. In any local area, a species does not arise gradually by the steady transformation of its ancestors; it appears all at once and "fully formed." (1977, 13, 14)

Niles Eldredge and Ian Tattersall agree by adding,

Expectation colored perception to such an extent that the *most obvious single fact about biological evolution—nonchange—*has seldom, if ever, been incorporated into anyone's scientific notions of how life actually evolves. If ever there was a myth, it is that evolution is a process of constant change. (1982, 8)

The gaps in the fossil record are being used by punctuationalists to support evolution, but it seems to a growing number of the populace watching the proceedings that punctuationalism is merely an ad hoc measure to bolster a collapsing evolutionary theory. A recent book by Michael Denton concludes that it would take "miracles" to bridge the discontinuities in the fossil record. He adds, "The punctuational model of Eldridge and Gould has been widely publicized but, ironically, while the theory was developed specifically to account for the absence of transitional varieties between species, its major effect seems to have been to draw widespread attention to the gaps in the fossil record" (Denton 1986, 194).

A Gallup poll in 1981 showed that nearly two-thirds of the people in a random survey believed in full-blown creation. For now the vast majority of these are nonscientists for whom the particular concern for proper scientific method is quite remote. But this could change when scientists begin to appreciate the two-domain approach to science, and thus the plausibility of primary-cause creation in origin science.

But is special creation really plausible? There is considerable circumstantial evidence for creation in the fossil record (the sudden appearance of fully formed fossils), but what about on balance (the successive-appearance feature of the fossil record)? The latter feature does readily fit the evolutionary view of descent with modification from some hypothetical common ancestor. Some young-earth creationists believe that the general pattern of fossil progression results from a universal flood where animals were layered in the debris according to their ability to survive the oncoming flood waters. Other young-earth creationists propose that fossil distribution into layers results from hydrodynamic sorting as remains settle out of violent flood waters.

Not all creationists share the young-earth view. Another large group, the progressive creationists, accept an old earth. The successive-appearance feature of the fossil record is taken by them as the order of introduction of creatures into the biosphere. Each major group was created in the sequence just as we see them in the fossil record. First invertebrates appeared; then a long period of stasis or time to equilibrate and fill out the ecosystem. Next to suddenly appear were fishes, then amphibia. After each burst of creation there was a period of calmness to let the disturbed ecosystem re-equilibrate. Later still the ruling reptiles were introduced, then birds and mammals, and eventually man was created.

The progressive-creation view does agree substantially with the fossil record. But there is no consensus among creationists. The age of the earth is the major difference, and this is hotly debated.* But the internal debate among creationists is a healthy sign that individual scientists are continuing the search for more plausible answers to the question of origins. Regardless of the way creationists resolve the questions of fossil distribution and the age of the earth, creationists agree that the sudden appearance of fully formed and functional creatures was the result of a primary cause. Thus the fossil record has provided circumstantial evidence for creation.

The overall case for creation will gain additional plausibility if a valid analogy between present and past is presented. Here we extend the argument about the origin of life. The great diversity of living forms is accepted by creationists to be an expression of the information resident in the DNA of each living form. The information defining a particular organism is taken as equivalent to the arrangement and sequence of nucleotides along the length of the DNA chain. Like fingerprints, the nucleotide sequences define a creature uniquely. Furthermore, the reproductive process transmits genetic characteristics from generation to generation. However, instead of reproduction being a genetic mixing bowl where all possible base sequences

*See Davis Young, *Christianity and the Age of the Earth* (1982) and Henry M. Morris, *Scientific Creationism* (1974).

are mixed, the mixing is constrained or limited in certain areas so that all the diverse creatures' types breed true. In other words, even though there is variation, cats give rise to cats, dogs give rise to dogs, and giraffes give rise to giraffes.

Creationists reason that because there are apparently real limits to genetic change, intelligent creation must have occurred for each major category of creatures (Lester and Bohlin 1984, chap. 8). Instead of a single nucleotide sequence being intelligently assembled, to be elaborated naturally into the great variety of life forms now evident, there was a whole suite of specific sequences assembled, each corresponding at least to the major categories of living things. The "mathematical identity" of the structures of nucleotide sequences and alphabetic letter sequences enables us to legitimately compare DNA to a written communication.

As specific letter sequences convey information (e.g., tomorrow is election day), so specific nucleotide sequences in DNA convey information to tell the cell how to make enzymes. The legitimacy of thinking about DNA in this way is significant because we know by experience that intelligence can manipulate letter sequences to convey information. Therein is a crucial point in a creationist argument for intelligent creation. For the principle of uniformity (analogy) means that the kinds of causes we observe producing certain kinds of effects today can be counted on to have produced similar effects in the past. The plausibility of "the present is the key to the past" arises from an observed constant conjunction of cause and effect. So it is concluded that if it takes intelligence to fashion English letters into "Mary had a little lamb" or the story of King Lear, then it is plausible to conclude an intelligent source arranged the nucleotide sequences in DNA for each major group of creatures. In the language of Hume, we judge by the regular observation of a "constant conjunction" between intelligence and a specific letter sequences that a similar intelligence produced the nucleotide sequence in the various categories in the living world.

Sagan has used the same kind of argument in showing that "a single message" from space would establish proof of extraterrestrial intelligence (1979, 275). Why then should we not accept an intelligent cause for the highly complex messages found in DNA?

The design argument in the nineteenth century was powerful, influencing all thinkers, not the least of whom was Darwin. Darwin could not avoid design; it was everywhere. But he did alter the way people thought about it, and thereby changed the intellectual climate of the entire Western world. He convinced the leading intellectuals of Europe and America that design is only apparent, having been the result of purely natural causes.

Now, however, the situation has taken a dramatic turn and so far few have recognized its significance. For the elucidation of the structure of DNA and unraveling the secrets of the genetic code have ushered in not only a new era of technology, but also the possibility of once again seeing true design in the universe.

Underneath all the biological structures which Darwin was persuaded merely manifested apparent design is DNA with its rich store of genetic information reflecting an intelligent source. So even if a satisfactory secondary-cause mechanism is found for generating information sequences in language systems or DNA, the view of a primary cause will remain plausible. For now it is the only plausible view. We are thus cast in a pre-Darwinian position where the universally observed design may be acknowledged as genuine. The words of Agassiz now speak as forcefully to us as they did to readers in 1860:

> [Darwin] has lost sight of the most striking of the features, and the one which pervades the whole, namely, that there runs throughout Nature unmistakable *evidence of thought*, corresponding to the mental operations of our own mind, and therefore intelligible to us as thinking beings, and unaccountable on any other basis than that they own their existence to the working of intelligence; and no theory that overlooks this element can be true to nature.

Summary and Conclusion

In conclusion, within the domain of origin science we have presented a case for plausibility of intelligent creation. It does not rest on analogy alone, for plausibility grows as we consider the circumstantial evidence of the fossils which testify to sudden appearance of full-blown creatures. We have not attempted a thorough survey of other evidences for primary-cause creation. Our central concern has been to show the formal structure for considering special creation as a valid part of science, by showing that it satisfies the criteria for origin science. Further, we have mapped out the beginnings of an approach to show the plausibility of primary-cause creation. Of course, this is only an outline. The detailed analysis is yet to be done by creationists. However, it seems clear that if creationist views are to gain scientific credibility, then they must follow the principles of origin science and build a positive case for a primary cause, rather than relying on the ineffective means of pointing out flaws in various evolutionary hypotheses.

Paley's Updated Argument

The following illustration is an updating of William Paley's famous watchmaker argument in the light of modern molecular biology and information theory. It deliberately borrows the format and language of Paley to make the point. It is an edited version of Norman L. Geisler's article which appeared in *Creation/Evolution* (Summer 1984, issue 13, vol. 4, no. 3) and was entitled "A Scientific Basis for Creation: The Principle of Uniformity."

In crossing a valley, suppose I come upon a round stratified stone and were asked how it came to be such. I might plausibly answer that it was once laid down by water in layers which later solidified by chemical action. One day it broke from a larger section of rock and was subsequently rounded by the natural erosional processes of tumbling in water. Suppose then, upon walking further, I come upon Mount Rushmore where the forms of four human faces appear on a granite cliff.[1] Even if I knew nothing about the origin of the faces, would I not come immediately to believe it was an intelligent production and not the result of natural processes of erosion?

Yet why should a natural cause serve for the stone but not for the faces? For this reason, namely, that when we come to inspect the faces on the mountain we perceive—what we could not discover in the stone—that they manifest intelligent contrivance, that they convey specifically complex information. The stone has redundant patterns or strata easily explainable by the observed natural process of sedimentation. The faces, however, have specially formed features, not merely repeated lines. The stone has rounded features like those we observe to result from natural erosion. The faces, on the other hand, have sharply defined features contrary to those made by erosion. In fact, the faces resemble things known to be made by intelligent artisans. These differences

---

1. I am indebted to Charles Thaxton for this illustration.

being observed, we would rightly conclude there must have existed at some time and at some place or other some intelligence that formed them.

Nor would it, I apprehend, weaken the conclusion if we had never seen such a face being chiseled in granite, that we had never known an artisan capable of making one, or that we were wholly incapable of executing such a piece of workmanship ourselves. All this is no more than what is true of some lost art or of some of the more curious productions of modern technology.

Neither, secondly, would it invalidate our conclusion that upon closer examination of the faces they turn out to be imperfectly formed. It is not necessary that a representation be perfect in order to show it was designed.

Nor, thirdly, would it bring any uncertainty in the argument if we were not able to recognize the identity of the faces. Even if we had never known of any such person portrayed, we would still conclude it took intelligence to produce them.

Nor, fourthly, would any man in his senses think the existence of the faces on the rock was accounted for by being told that they were one out of many possible combinations or forms rocks may take, and that this configuration might be exhibited as well as a different structure.

Nor, fifthly, would it yield our inquiry more satisfaction to be answered that there exists in granite a law or principle of order which had disposed it toward forming facial features. We never knew a sculpture made by such a principle of order, nor can we even form an idea of what is meant by such a principle of order distinct from intelligence.

Sixthly, we would be surprised to hear that configurations like this on a mountainside were not proof of intelligent creation but were only to induce the mind to think so.

Seventhly, we would be not less surprised to be informed that the faces resulted simply from the natural processes of wind and water erosion.

Nor, eighthly, would it change our conclusion were we to discover that certain natural objects or powers were utilized in producing the faces. Still the managing of these forces, the pointing and directing them to form such specific faces, demands intelligence.

Neither, ninthly, would it make the slightest difference in our conclusion were we to discover these natural laws were set up by some intelligent being. For nothing is added to the power of natural laws by positing an original designer for them. Designed or not, the natural powers of wind and rain erosion never produce human faces like this in granite.[2]

2. Even the principle of "natural selection" is never observed producing an entirely new form of life (see chap. 7). Natural selection is a principle known to be helpful in the conservation of existing organisms, but not in the production of totally new ones. Darwinians admit that the famous peppered-moth "experiments beautifully demonstrate natural selection—or survival of the fittest—in action. But they do not show evolution in progress. For however the populations may alter in their content of light, intermediate, or dark forms, all the moths remain from beginning to end *biston betularia.*"

Nor, tenthly, would it change the matter were we to discover that behind the forehead of a stone face was a computer capable of reproducing other faces on nearby cliffs by laser beams. This would only enhance our respect for the intelligence which designed such a computer.

And, furthermore, were we to find that this computer was designed by another computer we would still not give up our belief in an intelligent cause. In fact, we would have an even greater admiration for the intelligence it takes to create computers which can also create.

Further, would we not consider it strange if anyone suggested there was no need for an intelligent cause because there might be an infinite regress of computers designing computers? We know that increasing the number of computers in the series does not diminish the need for intelligence to program the whole series.

Neither would we allow any limitation on our conclusion (that it takes intelligence to create such specific and complex information) by the claim that this principle applies only to events of the near past but not the most remote past. For what is remote to us was near to those remote from us.

And would we not consider it arbitrary for anyone to insist that the word *science* applies to our reasoning only if we assume the face had a natural cause, such as erosion, but not if we conclude it had an intelligent source? For who would insist that an archaeologist is scientific only if he posits a non-intelligent natural cause of ancient pottery and tools?

Neither, lastly, would we be driven from our conclusion or from confidence in it by being told we know nothing at all about how the faces were produced. We know enough to conclude it took intelligence to produce them. The consciousness of knowing little need not beget a distrust of that which we do know. And we do know that natural forces never produce those kinds of effects. We know that the faces on the rock manifest a form such as is produced by intelligence. For as William Paley remarked, "wherever we see marks of contrivance, we are led for its cause to an *intelligent* author. And this transition of the understanding is found upon uniform experience."[3]

Now in like manner, suppose in exploring a cave we come upon a beautifully formed crystal. Would the order of its redundant patterns and the beauty of its symmetry lead us naturally to conclude it was formed by a creator? Not necessarily. Purely natural processes regularly produce such redundant order as is found in crystals.

Suppose also that in studying the genetic structure of a living organism, we discover that its DNA has a highly complicated and unique information code, distinguished by its specified complexity. Also, suppose we observe

L. Harrison Matthews, "Introduction," Charles Darwin, *Origin of Species* (London: Dent, 1971), p. xi.

3. See William Paley, *Natural Theology*, ed. Frederick Ferre (1802; New York: Bobbs-Merrill, 1963), p. 37.

that "living organisms are distinguished by their *specified complexity*. Crystals . . . fail to qualify as living because they lack *complexity*; random mixtures of polymers fail to qualify because they lack *specificity*."[4] Further, suppose we find that the specified information in even a single-celled organism is equal to that of one volume of an encyclopedia. Suppose, also, we discover that the information in living cells follows the same pattern as do combinations of letters used by intelligent beings to convey such information.[5] Suppose, further, we find that "nothing which even vaguely resembles a code [of life] exists in the physio-chemical world."[6] Noting all this, would we not conclude that it most probably took intelligence to produce a living organism? And would we not arrive at this position with the same degree of confidence with which we concluded that it took intelligence to inform the rock to take the specifically complex shape of a face?

And were we in addition to discover that the human brain contains more specific genetic information than the world's largest libraries, would we not consider most implausible any suggestion that the vast "library" of the brain might have emerged naturally from a more simple one-"volume" organism without intelligent intervention?[7]

Neither, I believe, would we be dissuaded from our conclusion of the strong likelihood of intelligent creation of the human mind by the fact that there are many other "books" in the library of living things with similar but less complex information. For experience indicates that such information in different books never transfers from one to another, either in the printing and shipping process, or as they come in contact on library shelves.

And it is doubtful whether any sensible person would change his convic-

---

4. Leslie Orgel, *The Origins of Life* (New York: Wiley, 1973), p. 189. Emphasis added.

5. Recently this interesting fact was brought to light by Hubert P. Yockey, who wrote: "The statistical structure of any printed language ranges through letter frequencies, diagrams, trigrams, word frequencies, etc., spelling rules, grammar and so forth and therefore can be represented by a Markov process given the states of the system. . . ." He adds that this same "sequence hypothesis applies directly to the protein and genetic text as well as to written language and therefore the treatment is mathematically identical." See "Self Organization Origin of Life Scenarios and Information Theory," *Journal of Theoretical Biology* (1981): 91.

6. Yockey shows that "the information content of modern proteins reflects a complexity nearly that of a random sequence. . . ." He adds, "The order in the naturally formed amino acid polymers is therefore an impediment and not a means of 'self organization' which leads to informational biomolecules and from thence to a genome." Ibid., p. 26.

7. Carl Sagan wrote, "The information content of the human brain expressed in bits is probably comparable to the total number of connections among the neurons— about a hundred trillion, 10^{14}, bits. If written out in English that information would fill some twenty million volumes, as many as in the world's largest libraries." *Cosmos* (New York: Random House, 1980), p. 278.

tion on these matters were it known that print is sometimes changed by natural processes (aging, damage). Nor would our view change if we heard stories that occasionally words leap inexplicably from one book to another. Still we are confident that such changes and transfers of print would take intelligent guidance to result in more complex information, not confusion. Uniform experience reveals that such information is never transformed from lower to higher forms except by intelligent intervention. For we know that even though all the words of *Hamlet* are in the Oxford Dictionary, nonetheless it takes intelligence to produce *Hamlet* out of the words in a dictionary.

Whence comes this assurance that such specifically complex information is caused by intelligence and that any such information transformation to higher codes takes intelligent manipulation? Is it not the "uniform experience" of all rational men? For has anyone ever observed an encyclopedia of information result from a fan blowing on alphabet cereal? Does making random mistakes in copying "Mary had a little lamb . . ." over long periods of time ever result in *Paradise Lost*? Do we ever observe either the origin or improvements in such complex information except by intelligent intervention?

Further, so firmly is the principle of uniformity established in our belief that we would be greatly surprised to hear that someone has put monkeys at typewriters, expecting them to produce a work of William Shakespeare,[8] or that someone is dropping marbles on a computer keyboard in the expectation of producing a superior program for it.

So certain are we that only minds convey specified complexity in information that when ancient inscriptions in unknown languages are discovered we do not hesitate to conclude some intelligent being inscribed them. And were astronomers to receive a decodeable message from outer space there would be no reason to conclude that it emanated from anything but an intelligent source.[9]

What is the basis of this confidence that it takes intelligence to originate such information? Is it not our uniform experience? And is it not true, to quote

8. The famous British astronomer Fred Hoyle recently concluded: "No matter how large the environment one considers, life cannot have had a random beginning. Troops of monkeys thundering away at random on typewriters could not produce the works of Shakespeare, for the practical reason that the whole observable universe is not large enough to contain the necessary monkey hordes, the necessary typewriters, and certainly the waste paper baskets required for the deposition of wrong attempts. The same is true for living material." Fred Hoyle and N. C. Wickramasinghe, *Evolution from Space* (London: Dent, 1981), p. 148.

9. Sagan wrote: "The receipt of a *single message* from space would show [earth dwellers] that it is possible to live through such technological adolescence [as we are now in]: the transmitting civilization, after all, has survived." See Carl Sagan, *Broca's Brain* (New York: Random House, 1979), p. 275, emphasis added.

David Hume, that "a *uniform experience* amounts to a proof, [so that] there is here a direct and full *proof* from the nature of the fact. . . ."[10]

In short, is not our belief in the high probability that intelligence produced the various complex information codes of living things based on the scientific principle of uniformity—"the present is the key to the past"? And since we did not observe the origin of living things, does it not follow that our speculations about these past events are entirely dependent on the trustworthiness of the principle of uniformity (analogy)? But in view of the fact that our experience uniformly indicates the need for intelligence to create such information, is not the hypothesis of a nonintelligent natural cause of living things contrary to the principle of uniformity on which scientific understanding of the past depends?

10. See David Hume, *An Enquiry Concerning Human Understanding*, ed. Charles W. Hendel (1748; New York: Bobbs-Merrill, 1955), p. 123.

Naturalism and Theism

There are two broad philosophical categories of thought: theism and naturalism. According to theism there is an absolute distinction between Creator and creation. In naturalism, however, an absolute distinction is denied, even if some kind of creator is acknowledged.

So belief systems are either theistic or naturalistic. Traditional Judaism, Islam, and Christianity are theistic religions since they make a radical distinction between Creator and creature. For example, a second-century definition of Christians described them as ones "who distinguish God from matter, and teaches [sic] that matter is one thing and God another" (cited in Aulie 1983, 426). Hinduism, Buddhism, and Secular Humanism are naturalistic religions admitting of no creator beyond the natural universe.

Within both broad categories of naturalism and theism there are some who believe that origin events result from the intervention of a primary cause (such as an intelligent creator) and others who hold that purely natural or secondary causes are adequate. The situation can be diagrammed as in figure 3.

Primary-Cause Theism (Theistic Creation)

Many within Judaism, Islam, and Christianity hold that origin events result from a supernatural intervention of a primary cause; that is, an intelligent Creator. Proponents of "creation science," as well as others (including the authors), fall into this category and are generally called creationists. Until the eighteenth century there were few who held that only primary causality was

FIGURE 3

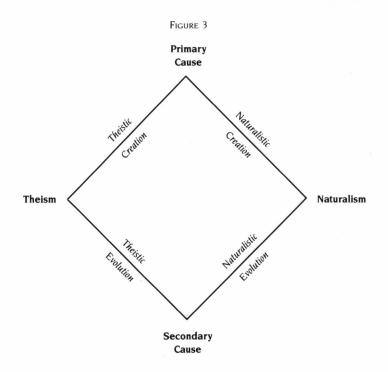

involved in origins. It is true that many important Christian thinkers through history (e.g., Augustine, Anselm, and Thomas Aquinas) held that primary causation was involved in origins. But such theists did not always argue for the exclusivity of primary causes. Richard Aulie (1983, 418–62) provides evidence that Europeans placed no particular emphasis on the difference between primary and secondary causes until the eighteenth century. Nearly everyone believed God created the world and life, but many were not particularly concerned with how he did it. So to label historic theism a view involving only primary causality is not accurate. And to say a secondary-cause view is not a historic theistic view is also an error, for Augustine held a form of it. It would be more accurate to say that historically the question of how God performed all his creative acts was not a central concern until the eighteenth century. It crystallized into a major issue in the nineteenth century (the post-Darwinian era), and the controversy has continued unabated since that time.

Historical scholarship shows that in the nineteenth century the secondary-cause view was sanctioned by many in the church (see Moore 1979). And as Moore has shown, the conflict over how God created did not start immediately. But by century's end and throughout the twentieth century the origins issue has been very divisive in the church, as it has been in Judaism and Islam.

Secondary-Cause Theism (Theistic Evolution)

This view also holds to a theistic view of God, but stresses that God created through natural processes, or secondary causes. Over the course of the last century a number of well-known orthodox Christians have held this view. Asa Gray, the famous Harvard botanist, said in 1876 that he was "a Darwinian," and that "philosophically a convinced theist, and religiously an acceptor of the 'creed commonly called the Nicene,' as the exponent of the Christian faith" (Aulie 1983, 419–20). Other theists who believed God used secondary causes include A. A. Hodge (son of Charles Hodge), A. H. Strong, and surprisingly many authors of *The Fundamentals* (1910–15) who helped start the modern fundamentalist movement (such as B. B. Warfield, James Orr, and George Wright).

Proponents of secondary-cause theism believe in some form of evolution. But because they are theists, some prefer to call themselves creationists. In the light of this, the ambiguity attending the use of the terms *creationist* and *evolutionist* is evident. Thus, simply labeling one a creationist does not tell whether one is espousing primary or secondary causes, or affirming theism or naturalism. Describing one as an evolutionist is a bit less vague. It does at least identify one as using secondary causes. But by itself it is insufficient to determine whether one is affirming theism or naturalism. Calling oneself a primary- or secondary-cause theist is perhaps more cumbersome, but it is clear.

The difficulty of labeling one a primary- or secondary-cause theist comes in considering how many acts of primary or supernatural creation there were. One helpful way is to consider three basic categories of origin events: the origin of the universe, of life, and of new life forms (including man). The chart (table 2) will help clarify the issue.

There is wide though not universal agreement that the "total-creation" view is rightly labeled creation, and "total evolution" is appropriately called evolution. But it is somewhat arbitrary or a matter of personal preference as to whether "basic creation" should be called that or "basic evolution" or the reverse, since those who ascribe to these views both believe that some origin events result from a primary cause and some from a secondary cause.

The "purists" in the creationist camp are the total creationists. There is a tendency on their part to classify anyone else as evolutionists. This is not accurate. For total creationists, basic creationists, and basic evolutionists all believe in primary-cause creation. Likewise, it is misleading to call only "total evolutionists" by the term *evolutionists*, since basic creationists, basic evolutionists, and total evolutionists all believe in secondary-cause evolution of something(s).

Primary-Cause Naturalism (Naturalistic Creation)

This view holds that there is a creator of life which is *within* the natural universe, not beyond it. So life does not arise by purely secondary causes, but only by a primary-cause intervention. Fred Hoyle and N. C. Wickramasinghe presented this view of the origin of life (1981). Indeed, many Hindus and Buddhists hold this position. Sometimes proponents of this view argue on the side of primary-cause supernatural creationists (theistic creationists) against various degrees of secondary-cause evolution, whether naturalistic or theistic. However, there is an important difference between primary-cause naturalism and primary-cause theism. The former believes the Creator is within nature and the latter holds the Creator is beyond the universe. One usually finds primary-cause naturalism associated with pantheism or pan-entheism (see Geisler 1984, chaps. 4–5).

Secondary-Cause Naturalism (Naturalistic Evolution)

This position holds that all origin events resulted by purely secondary (natural) causes. Those who hold this view are called evolutionists though many are religious and a few even believe in some form of deity. Usually the proponents of this position are either atheists, agnostics, or deists (ibid., chaps. 3, 6). T. H. Huxley and Charles Darwin were notable proponents of this view.

Now the creation-evolution controversy is most often between primary-cause theism (theistic creationism) and secondary-cause naturalism (naturalistic evolutionism), though the other two positions are distinctive alternatives. Since primary-cause naturalists also believe in a "creator" they too are creationists of a kind, as opposed to secondary-cause naturalists, who claim there are only secondary causes of origin events.

Likewise, since secondary-cause theists often admit to at least one (or two) acts of a primary cause, they too can be appropriately called creationists. The major distinction between them and the primary-cause supernaturalists is in how many direct supernatural creative acts there were. The main difference today is that most secondary-cause theists (theistic evolutionists) accept natural (secondary) causes for all living organisms.

The most basic issues, however, seem to be whether or not to admit primary causes into science, and if so whether to admit the possibility of a supernatural primary cause. Both of these characteristics are unique to

TABLE 2

Creationist and Evolutionist Views

	Creationists			
	Total Creation	*Basic Creation*	*Basic Evolution*	*Total Evolution*
Primary Cause	Universe Life New Forms	Universe Life	Universe	
Secondary Cause		New Forms	Life New Forms	Universe Life New Forms
		Evolutionists		

primary-cause supernaturalists and are at the heart of the creation-evolution controversy.

Although these four basic views of origins (table 2) are clearly manifest among contemporary writers, it is important to consider whether or not it is proper to admit primary causes into science. We have tried to make the case for an affirmative answer to this question (see chaps. 6–7). If one considers the concept of two-domain science, that is, origin science and operation science, then it is possible to allow primary causes in origin science while limiting operation science to secondary causes. Operation science will contiue to be restricted to secondary causes. And since a primary cause of the origin of the whole natural world has been made plausible via the big bang theory, there is no reason to forbid the introduction of a supernatural cause of other origin events, such as the origin of life and new life forms. Indeed, this is precisely where modern science began (see chap. 2).

Miracles and Primary Causality

According to origin science it is plausible to posit a supernatural primary cause for the origin of the universe, the origin of life, and the origin of new life forms (including man). These are singularities and as such do not come under the domain of operation science, which deals with regularities. Hence the plausibility of postulating a primary supernatural cause for these origin singularities is not tested by measuring the hypothesis against a recurring pattern of events in nature. Rather it is judged in terms of the principles such as causality and uniformity (analogy) (see chap. 6). If constant conjunction in the present reveals that it takes a primary cause to produce a certain kind of effect (e.g., specified complexity of information), then it is assumed that the same is true of a similar effect in the past. Thus origin science is capable of handling past singularities by means of the principle of uniformity.

Although emphasis has been placed on the ability of science to deal with past singularities (origin science), science is also capable of treating singularities in the present. In other words, the same logic which applies to origin science also applies to the question of miracles in the present. That is, whether a rare occurrence in the present is an anomaly (with an unknown natural cause) or a miracle (with a supernatural cause), it is still the subject of singularity science. It is our proposal here that miracles fall into the class of singularity science in the present, just as creation is an example of a singularity science in the past (see introduction and chap. 6). And if a single event conveys specifically complex information, then it may be assumed to have a primary (intelligent) cause. For a naturalist has no scientific grounds for assuming a present singularity is naturally caused unless it can be shown to be part of a recurring pattern of events. If it can, then by definition it has a secondary cause. But if it is not known to be part of a regularly recurring pattern, then it may have a primary cause.

What is necessary for a theist to establish a singularity as a miracle is to

171

show that it fits into a complex information-conveying context. If it can be shown to convey specified and complex information, then by analogy (the principle of uniformity) the theist has justification to posit a primary cause for it. For example, the letters *SOS* in one's alphabet cereal convey no message. But if the context changes, then the same letters can convey a significant message. For these same letters in Morse code received on a ship radio during a storm are plausibly interpreted as a distress signal. Likewise, if a theist can show that a given singularity in a specific theistic context conveys divine information then it can be plausibly interpreted as a "message" from God (see Geisler 1982b, chap. 9). Such is the nature of miracles recorded in the Bible. There was a "sermon" in the sign, a "message" in the miracle. The unusual event said something to those who understood the theistic context in which it was given. Of course to those outside the theistic context, the event seems as devoid of a primary intelligent cause as the three letters *SOS* juxtaposed in his alphabet cereal. A good example of this is when the same phenomenon was interpreted as the voice of God by theists and as thunder by naturalists (John 12:29). The context made the difference.*

Some events, of course, will not have telltale characteristics of having either a secondary or a primary cause. That is, it might be difficult to prove they are part of an overall recurring pattern (as meteors once were). Likewise, one might not be able to give convincing evidence even to other theists that the event fits into an overall context of a message from God. For example, a sudden recovery from sickness is not always a divine healing. Natural remissions of illness sometimes happen quickly too. In such cases whether there is a primary cause of the event will remain open to dispute (and mere belief) until more definitive data are available to establish it as either a natural or a miraculous event. In the meantime the naturalist has no plausible grounds to insist the singularity has a natural cause, unless or until he can give reason to see it as part of a recurring pattern of natural events. And, likewise, the supernaturalist has no justification for claiming this event has a supernatural intelligent cause unless or until he can show that it fits into a context which conveys intelligent information. The event simply remains anomalous.

In order for either theist or naturalist to justifiably claim a certain kind of cause he must present evidence for that kind of cause. Evidence that it is naturally caused will be the kind which shows how it fits into a recurring pattern of events in nature. Evidence that it had an intelligent cause will need to show that the event conveys intelligent information from a superhuman source. Whether a superhuman intelligent cause is within nature or beyond

---

*This would also apply to supernormal primary causes which Christians identify as demons. In order to determine if a primary intelligent cause is an evil spirit there must be some telltale signs of evil that are discernible from the context (see Geisler 1982b, chap. 9).

(and, therefore, supernatural) will be determined by whether it can be identified with a primary cause of the natural (material) world. Historically, many of the early scientists made such an identification. And in the light of big bang cosmogony there is no reason such an identification cannot be made by scientists today as well. Likewise, if such a primary cause exists which "created heaven and earth," then there is no reason to assume that he cannot intervene in the universe. What remains is to identify a rare event conveying intelligent information from such a primary cause. Then the event would qualify as a miracle.

U.S. Court of Appeals Dissenting Opinion on the Louisiana Creation-Evolution Law

Thomas Gibbs Gee, Circuit Judge, with whom Charles Clark, Chief Judge, Thomas M. Reavley, Will Garwood, Patrick E. Higginbotham, Robert M. Hill and Edith H. Jones, Circuit Judges, join dissenting:

Today |Dec. 12, 1985| our full court approves, by declining review en banc, a panel opinion striking down a Louisiana statute as one "respecting an establishment of religion." The panel reasons that by requiring public school teachers to present a balanced view of the current evidence regarding the origins of life and matter (if any view is taught) rather than that favoring one view only and by forbidding them to misrepresent as established fact views on the subject which today remain theories only, the statute promotes religious belief and violates the academic freedom of instructors to teach whatever they like.

The *Scopes* court upheld William Jennings Bryan's view that states could constitutionally forbid teaching the scientific evidence for the theory of evolution, rejecting that of Clarence Darrow that truth was truth and could always be taught—whether it favored religion or not. By requiring that the whole truth be taught, Louisiana aligned itself with Darrow; striking down that requirement, the panel holding aligns us with Bryan.

I disagree with this holding; and because we endorse it today, I respectfully dissent.

Background

In 1981 the Louisiana legislature passed the legislation which is the subject of today's controversy. Sections 17:286.1 through 286.7, Louisiana Revised Statutes. Its full text appears as an appendix to the panel opinion, at 765 F.2d 1251, 1258. The general purport of this law is to provide three things:

175

1. That the "subject of origins" of the universe, of life, and of species need not be taught at all in the public schools of Louisiana; but,
2. That if *either* "creation-science" (defined as "the scientific evidences for creation and inferences from" them) *or* "evolution-science" (parallel definition) be taught, balanced treatment be given the other; and,
3. That, if taught, each be taught as a theory, "rather than as proven scientific fact."

I am as capable as the panel of making an extra-record guess that much, if not most, of the steam which drove this enactment was generated by religious people who were hostile to having the theory of evolution misrepresented to school children as established scientific fact and who wished the door left open to acceptance by these children of the Judeo-Christian religious doctrine of Divine Creation. If so, however, they did not seek to further their aim by requiring that religious doctrine be taught in public school. Instead, they chose a more modest tactic—one that I am persuaded does not infringe the Constitution.

That was to provide, as my summary of the statute indicates, that neither evolution nor creation be presented as finally established scientific fact and that, when evolution is taught as a theory, the scientific evidence for such competing theories as a "big bang" production of the universe or for the sudden appearance of highly developed forms of life be given equal time (and vice versa). As I noted at the outset, the record contains affidavits—some of them by highly qualified scientists who there proclaim themselves agnostics and believers in evolution as a theory—which affirm that the above propositions are correct: that evolution is not established fact and that there is strong evidence that life and the universe came about in a different manner, one perhaps less inconsistent with religious doctrine. At the least, these affidavits make a fact issue that those propositions are true. For purposes of reviewing the summary judgment which our panel's opinion affirms, then, the propositions stated must be taken as established: there *are* two bona fide views.

It follows that the Louisiana statute requires no more than that neither theory about the origins of life and matter be misrepresented as fact, and that if scientific evidence supporting either view of how these things came about be presented in public schools, that supporting the other must be—so that within the reasonable limits of the curriculum, the subject of origins will be discussed in a balanced manner if it is discussed at all. I see nothing illiberal about such a requirement, nor can I imagine that Galileo or Einstein would have found fault with it. Indeed, so far as I am aware even Ms. O'Hair has never asked for more than equal time.

Let it be conceded, for purposes of argument, that many of those who worked to get this legislation passed did so with a religious motive. It well may be that many who advocated Louisiana's Sunday closing Law, recently upheld by us, did so from such a motive. There being evident a credible secular purpose for that law, however, we upheld it. *Home Depot, Inc. v. Guste*, No. 84–3532, slip op. at 167 (Oct. 10, 1985). There can be no doubt that the Louisiana Legislature was empowered under the state constitution to enact the law in question, one mandating a particular course of public school instruction; the Louisiana Supreme Court has squarely so held, on certification from us earlier in the course of this appeal. *Aguillard v. Treen*, 440 So.2d 704 (La. 1983).

Despite this, our panel struck the statute down.

The Panel Opinion

The panel's reasoning is simple. *Lemon v. Kurtzman*, 403 U.S. 602 (1971), sets three hurdles before any statute attacked as establishing religion. The panel holds that the Louisiana statute trips over the first, which requires that "the statute must have a secular legislative purpose; . . . ." *Lemon, supra*, at 612. I cannot agree.

The panel opinion chiefly rests upon such Supreme Court authorities as *Lemon* (state aid to church schools), *Stone v. Graham*, 449 U.S. 39 (1980) (posting Ten Commandments in every classroom), and *Wallace v. Jaffree*, ___ U.S. ___, 86 L.Ed.2d 29 (1985) (moment of silence for "meditation or voluntary prayer"), as well as on such holdings from our own court as *Lubbock Civil Liberties Union v. Lubbock I.S.D.*, 669 F2d 1038 (5th Cir. 1982) (religious meetings on school property) and *Karen B. v. Treen*, 653 F2d 897 (5th Cir. 1981) (classroom prayer). Such authorities treat of statutes having a direct and clear religious connection, either by way of granting public assistance to religious schools or by requiring or permitting religious activities in public ones. The statute which concerns us today is quite different: it has no direct religious reference whatever and merely requires that the whole scientific truth be taught on the subject if any is.

In order to invalidate it as "establishing religion," it was therefore necessary for the panel to look beyond the statute's words and beyond legislative statements of secular purpose. To strike the statute down, the panel drew upon its visceral knowledge regarding what must have motivated the legislators. It sifts their hearts and minds, divines their motive for requiring that truth be taught, and strikes down the law that requires it. This approach effactually makes a farce of the judicial exercise of discerning legislative intent. The task is admittedly a most difficult and often impossible one, since legislatures are not known for providing clear guidance to those interpreting their works; but it is a task constitutionally required. To disregard so completely the existing manifestations of intent and impose instead one's personal, subjective ideas as to what *must* have been the true sentiment of the Louisiana legislature ignores this constitutional restraint on judicial power.

Moreover, even assuming the panel's guess about legislative sentiment is right, the informity of its reasoning becomes immediately evident when it is extended from prescribing what is to be taught to the teaching itself. If it is unconstitutional to *require* secular matter to be taught from a motive to advance religion it must necessarily also be unconstitutional to *teach* it from such a motive. If so, a public school teacher so indiscreet as to admit to teaching the evidence for creation science from a motive to advance religion is subject to being silenced, while one teaching exactly the same matter without such a motive cannot be interfered with. Like a clock that strikes 13, a rule that produces such a result as this cannot be sound.

I await with interest the application of this new mode of constitutional analysis to other statutes. The bigamy laws, for example, carry tell-tale indicia of having been passed with a motive to favor the Judeo-Christian religious preference for monogamy, singling it out for adoption over the equally workable Moslem view. Perhaps our court, consulting its intuitive knowledge about what motivates legislators, will presently determine that there can be no secular purpose in such a preferment of one model of the marital relationship over another, especially when the effect of doing so is to espouse the religious doctrine of the two larger religious sects in our country over that of the minority of Moslems. But such intriguing possibilities must await another day, and I return to the case in hand.

I should have thought that requiring the truth to be taught on any subject displayed its own secular warrant, one at the heart of the scientific method itself. Put another way, I am surprised to learn that a state cannot forbid the teaching of half-truths in its public schools, whatever its motive in doing so. Today we strike down a statute balanced and fair on its face because of our perception of the reason why it got the votes to pass: one to prevent the closing of children's minds to religious doctrine by misrepresenting it as in conflict with established scientific laws. After today, it does not suffice to teach the truth; one must also teach it with the approved motive. It may be that the Constitution forbids a state to require the teaching of lies in the classrooms of its public schools; perhaps among its emanations or penumbras there can be found means to invalidate such a law, say, as one mandating that students be taught that the earth is flat or that chattel slavery never existed in this country. It comes as news to me, however, that the Constitution forbids a state to require the teaching of truth—any truth, for any purpose, and whatever the effect of teaching it may be. Because this is the holding that we endorse today, I decline to join in that endorsement and respectfully dissent.

APPENDIX **5**

A Greek Versus a Modern View of Science*

	Greek Science	Modern Science
Method	Define essence (form)	Describe activity (law)
	Deduce properties	Relate activities
	Syllogistic	Systematic
	Contemplation and deduction	Observation and experimentation
	Sensible is not knowable	Sensible is knowable
	Empirical used for *illustrations*	Empirical used for *evidence*†
Nature	Sensible is not real	Sensible is real
	Form (not matter) is real	Matter is real
	Matter corrupts form	Matter does not corrupt form
	Nature (form) is necessary	Nature is contingent
	Nature is uncreated	Nature is created
God	God is limited by nature	God is unlimited by nature
	Director of nature	Creator of nature
	Final (or formal) cause	Efficient cause
	No control over nature	Complete control over nature
	Creation is necessary	Creation is voluntary

*This chart is based on distinctions made by M. B. Foster (1934).

†Not until the empirical became indispensable to a knowledge of nature was the way paved for modern science. According to Edward B. Davis, Jr., this was influenced by a Christian view that God freely created the world. He wrote, "My conclusion is that Foster was correct, at least from the individuals I have studied [Galileo, Descartes, Boyle, and Newton]. Theology impugned on natural philosophy through the doctrine of creation, . . . an emphasis on the divine will went hand in hand with a belief in the primacy of phenomena; a lack of emphasis on the divine will was accompanied by an *a priori* attitude toward nature" (1984, 23b).

Summary of Creation Evidence*

Aspect of Creation Science	Affirmative Evidence	Testable Claim
Biological creation	Paleontology	The fossil record is generally characterized by an abrupt appearance of complex genera/families and higher categories and by systematic gaps between such fossil categories.
	Comparative morphology	The structure of fossilized organisms generally is systematically similar to their modern-day counterparts and generally exhibits systematic stasis until the present or their extinction.
	Information content	The information content of all organisms, including their complex features and molecules, is sufficiently vast to render biological creation plausible and biological macroevolution extremely implausible.
	Probability	The mathematical probability is higher for biological creation and vastly low for biological macroevolution of complex features, complex organs, and symbiotic organisms.
	Genetics	Genetic limits on the scope and frequency of viable mutations generally restrict viable variation or

*This material is summarized from a brief presented to the U.S. Supreme Court (Dec. 10, 1986) by Wendell Bird, lead counsel, in opposition to the ACLU motion for summary judgment (pursuant to Fed. R. Civ. P. 56 (c) and E. D. La. R. 3. 10, pp. 384–86).

181

Aspect of Creation Science	Affirmative Evidence	Testable Claim
		microevolution, provide genetic barriers between genera/families, and prevent biological macroevolution.
	Comparative unrelated-ness	Anomalies in classification, comparative anatomy, and comparative biochemistry are sufficiently extensive as to point more plausibly to distinct ancestry than common ancestry of various genera/families.
Biochemical creation	Information content	The information content of the least complex organisms and their genetic coding systems are sufficiently vast to render biochemical creation plausible and biochemical evolution extremely implausible.
	Probability	The mathematical probability is higher for biochemical creation and vastly low for biochemical evolution of the least complex organisms and of their enzymes, other proteins, and DNA.
	Isomers	The isomers in protein amino acids and nucleic acid sugars would not plausibly have arisen in a primordial soup, but are generally necessary to life and are more plausibly explained by biochemical creation.
	Chemistry	The general chemical tendency outside of a living organism is away from life and away from molecules necessary for life rather than toward life.
	Thermo-dynamics	The thermodynamic probability of the first life is higher for biochemical creation and vastly low for biochemical evolution.
Cosmic creation	Thermo-dynamics	The first and second laws of thermodynamics require a beginning for the universe and preclude its eternal existence.
	Radiohalos	The polonium halos in the earth's crust require an abruptly appearing and initially cool earth, in the absence of uranium or thorium halos.
	Information content	The information content of the universe is sufficiently vast to render cosmic

Aspect of Creation Science	Affirmative Evidence	Testable Claim
		creation plausible and cosmic evolution extremely implausible.
	Hetero-geneity	The heterogeneity of the universe is implausible under the big bang hypothesis and is more plausibly explained by cosmic creation.
	Star and galaxy formation	The formation of galactic clusters, galaxies, stars, and the solar system requires extremely improbable conditions or is not explainable by but contrary to natural laws, and is more plausibly explained by cosmic creation.

Bibliography

Abel, Ernest L. 1973. *Ancient views on the origins of life.* Rutherford, N.J.: Fairleigh Dickinson University Press.

Adler, Irving. 1957. *How life began.* New York: Signet.

Adler, Mortimer J. [1967] 1968. *The difference of man and the difference it makes.* New York: Meridian.

Agassiz, Louis. 1860. Contribution to the natural history of the United States. *American Journal of Science.*

Anderson, J. Kerby. 1980. *Life, death, and beyond.* Grand Rapids: Zondervan.

———. 1982. *Genetic engineering.* Grand Rapids: Zondervan.

Anderson, J. Kerby, and Harold Coffin. 1977. *Fossils in focus.* Grand Rapids: Zondervan.

Aristotle. 1941. *The basic works of Aristotle.* Ed. Richard McKeon. New York: Random House.

Armstrong, D. M. 1978. *A theory of universals.* Vol. 2. Cambridge: Cambridge University Press.

Asimov, Isaac. 1981, October. The genesis war. *Science Digest.*

Aulie, Richard P. 1983. Evolution and special creation: Historical aspects of the controversy. *Proceedings of the American Philosophical Society,* 127(6).

Bacon, Francis. [1620] 1960. *The new organon and related writings.* Ed. Fulton H. Anderson. New York: Bobbs-Merrill.

Barbour, Ian G. 1966. *Issues in science and religion.* Englewood Cliffs, N.J.: Prentice-Hall.

Bell, Eric T. 1937. *Men of mathematics.* New York: Simon and Schuster.

Berry, Richard W. 1983. The beginning. In *Is God a creationist?* Ed. Roland M. Frye. New York: Scribner.

Bird, Wendell. 1984. Brief of the state [of Louisiana] in opposition to ACLU motion for summary judgment. Vol. 1, Civil Action No. 81–4787.

Blum, Harold F. 1951. *Time's arrow and evolution.* Princeton, N.J.: Princeton University Press.

Bradley, Walter L. 1984. The trustworthiness of Scripture in areas relating to natural science. In *Hermeneutics, inerrancy, and the Bible*. Ed. Earl D. Radmacher and Robert D. Preus. Grand Rapids: Zondervan, Academie Books.

Brandon, S. G. F. 1963. *Creation legends of the ancient Near East*. London: Hodder and Stoughton.

Bube, Richard H. 1978. The failure of the God-of-the-gaps. In *Horizons of science*. Ed. Carl F. H. Henry. New York: Harper and Row.

Buffon, Georges Louis Leclerc de. 1797. *Buffon's natural history: Containing a theory of the earth*. 10 vols. London: n.p. Vol. 1.

Burnet, John. [1892] 1967. *Early Greek philosophy*. New York: Meridian.

Butler, Joseph. 1900. *The analogy of religion*. New York: Macmillan.

Butterfield, Herbert. [1951] 1957. *The origins of modern science. 1300–1800*. New York: The Free Press.

Chambers, Robert. [1844] 1969. *Vestiges of the natural history of creation*. Leicester: Leicester University Press.

Chryssides, George D. 1975, September 11. Miracles and agents. *Religious Studies*.

Craig, William L. 1986. God, creation and Mr. Davies. *British Journal of Philosophy of Science* 37:163–75.

Creation/Evolution [journal]. Buffalo, N.Y.

Darwin, Charles. [1871] 1896. *The descent of man and selection in relation to sex*. New York: D. Appleton and Company.

———. [1859] 1958. *On the origin of species*. New York: New American Library.

Darwin, Francis. 1888. *The life and letters of Charles Darwin*. 3 vols. London: John Murray.

Davies, Paul. 1984. *Superforce*. New York: Simon and Schuster.

Davis, Edward B., Jr. 1984. *Creation, contingency, and early modern science*. Ann Arbor: University Microfilms International.

Denton, Michael. 1986. *Evolution: A theory in crisis*. New York: Adler and Adler.

Descartes, René. [1637] 1956. *Discourse on method*. Trans. Lawrence J. Lafleur. New York: Bobbs-Merrill.

Diamond, Malcolm L. 1973. Miracles. *Religious Studies* 9.

Dobzhansky, Theodosius. 1965. *The origins of prebiological systems and their molecular matrices*. Ed. S. W. Fox. New York: Academic.

Doolittle, Russell. 1981, October 13. Scientific creation/scientific evolution debate. Liberty Baptist College, Lynchburg, Va.

Draper, John W. 1897. *History of the conflict between religion and science*. New York: D. Appleton and Company.

Edwards, Paul, ed. 1967. *The encyclopedia of philosophy*. Vols. 1–8. New York: Macmillan and The Free Press.

Eiseley, Loren. 1957. *The immense journey*. New York: Vintage.

Eldredge, Niles. 1982. *The monkey business*. New York: Washington Square Press.

Eldredge, Niles, and Ian Tattersall. 1982. *The myths of human evolution*. New York: Columbia University Press.

Fisher, Robert B. 1981. *God did it, but how?* Grand Rapids: Zondervan, Academie Books.

Flew, Antony. 1967a. *Evolutionary ethics.* New York: St. Martin's Press.

––––––. 1967b. Miracles. In *The encyclopedia of philosophy.* Ed. Paul Edwards. New York: Macmillan and The Free Press, 5:346–53.

Flew, Antony, and Alasdair MacIntyre, eds. 1955. *New essays in philosophical theology.* New York: Macmillan.

Foote, Henry Wilder. 1947. *Thomas Jefferson.* Boston: Beacon.

Foster, M. B. 1934. The Christian doctrine of creation and the rise of modern natural science. *Mind,* 43.

Friar, Wayne, and Percival Davis. 1983. *A case for creation.* Chicago: Moody.

Frye, Roland M., ed. 1983. *Is God a creationist?* New York: Scribner.

Fundamentals. 1910–15. Chicago: Testimony Publishing Company.

Futuyma, Douglas J. 1982. *Science on trial.* New York, Pantheon.

Galilei, Galileo. 1965. Letter to Her Ladyship Christine of Lorraine Grand Duchess of Tuscany (1615). In *The works of Galileo Galilei.* Vol. 5. Florence: G. Barbera.

Geisler, Norman L. 1982a. *The Creator in the courtroom.* Milford, Mich.: Mott Media.

––––––. 1982b. *Miracles and modern thought.* Grand Rapids: Zondervan.

––––––. 1983a. The scientific inadequacies of Secular Humanism. In *Is man the measure?* Grand Rapids: Baker.

––––––. 1983b. Should creation science be taught in the public schools? *National Council on Religion and Public Schools.* Vol. 10, no. 3.

Geisler, Norman L., and William D. Watkins. 1984. *Perspectives.* San Bernardino, Calif.: Here's Life Publishers.

Gilkey, Langdon. 1959. *Maker of heaven and earth.* Garden City, N.Y.: Doubleday.

––––––. 1970. *Religion and the scientific future.* New York: Harper and Row.

––––––. 1981. Oral deposition of Dr. Langdon Gilkey. The United States District Court, Eastern District of Arkansas, Western Division.

––––––. 1982. The theologian's case against creationism: A conversation with Langdon Gilkey. *Reader* 11(23).

––––––. 1985. *Creationism on trial.* Minneapolis: Winston.

Gillespie, Neal. 1979. *Charles Darwin and the problems of creation.* Chicago: University of Chicago Press.

Gillispie, Charles Coulston. [1951] 1959. *Genesis and geology.* New York: Harper and Brothers.

Gish, Duane T. 1973. *Evolution? The Fossils Say No!* San Diego: Creation-Life Publishers.

Glass, Bentley, ed. 1959. *Forerunners of Darwin: 1745–1859.* Baltimore: Johns Hopkins Press.

Godfrey, Laurie R., ed. 1983. *Scientists confront creationism.* New York: Norton.

Gould, Stephen Jay. 1977, May. Evolution's erratic pace. *Natural History.*

Grinnell, George. 1972, May. Reexamination of the foundations. *Pensee.*

Henry, Carl F. H., ed. 1978. *Horizons of science.* New York: Harper and Row.

Herschel, John F. W. |1830| 1851. *Preliminary discourse on the study of natural philosophy*. London: Longman, Brown, Green and Longmans.

Himmelfarb, Gertrude. 1962. *Darwin and the Darwinian revolution*. New York: Doubleday.

Hitching, Francis. 1982. *The neck of the giraffe*. New Haven: Ticknor and Fields.

Hobbes, Thomas. |1651| 1952. *Leviathan*. Great books of the western world series. Ed. Robert M. Hutchins. Vol. 23. Chicago: Encyclopaedia Britannica.

Holton, Gerald. 1973. *Thematic origins of scientific thought*. Cambridge, Mass.: Harvard University Press.

———. 1982. Editorial. *Science, Technology, and Human Values*, 7(40).

Hoyle, Fred, and N. C. Wickramasinghe. 1981. *Evolution from space*. London: Dent.

Hume, David. 1932. Letter to John Stuart. In *Letters of David Hume*. Ed. J. Y. T. Greig. 2 vols. Oxford: Clarendon.

———. |1748| 1955. *An inquiry concerning human understanding*. Ed. Charles W. Hendel. New York: Bobbs-Merrill.

———. |1779| 1957. *Dialogues concerning natural religion*. Ed. Henry D. Aiken. New York: Hafner.

Hummel, Charles E. 1986. *The Galileo connection*. Downers Grove, Ill.: Inter-Varsity.

Hutton, James. 1795. *Theory of the earth with proofs and illustrations*. Vols. 1, 2. Edinburgh: Cadell, Junior, and Davies.

Huxley, Julian. 1953. *Evolution in action*. New York: Penguin.

———. 1957. *Religion without revelation*. New York: Mentor.

Jastrow, Robert. 1977. *Until the sun dies*. New York: Norton.

———. 1978. *God and the astronomers*. New York: Norton.

———. 1982, August 6. A scientist caught between two faiths. *Christianity Today*.

Kant, Immanuel. |1783| 1950. *Prolegomena to any future metaphysics*. New York: Bobbs-Merrill.

———. |1788| 1956. *Critique of practical reason*. New York: Bobbs-Merrill.

———. |1793| 1960. *Religion within the limits of reason alone*. New York: Harper and Row.

———. |1781| 1965. *Critique of pure reason*. New York: St. Martin's Press.

———. |1755| 1968. Universal natural history and the theory of the heavens. In *Kant's cosmogony*. Ed. Willy Ley. Trans. W. Haste. New York: Greenwood.

Kenny, Anthony. 1969. *The five ways: St. Thomas Aquinas' proofs of God's existence*. New York: Schocken.

Keosian, J. 1964. *The origin of life*. New York: Reinhold.

Kirk, G. S., and J. E. Raven. 1957. *The presocratic philosophers*. Cambridge: Cambridge University Press.

Kitcher, Philip. 1982. *Abusing science*. Cambridge, Mass.: MIT Press.

Klaaren, Eugene M. 1977. *Religious origins of modern science*. Grand Rapids: Eerdmans.

Kline, A. David. 1983. Theories, facts, and gods: Philosophical aspects of the creation-evolution controversy. In *Did the devil make Darwin do it?* Ed. David B. Wilson. Ames, Iowa: Iowa State University Press.

Koyre, Alexandre. 1968. *From the closed world to the infinite universe.* Baltimore: Johns Hopkins Press.

Kuhn. Thomas S. 1970. *The structure of scientific revolutions.* 2d ed. Vols. 1, 2. International Encyclopedia of Unified Science. Chicago: University of Chicago Press.

Kurtz, Paul. 1973. *Humanist manifestos I and II.* Buffalo: Prometheus.

Laplace, Pierre Simon de. |1796| 1830. *The system of the world.* Vols. 1–2. London: Longman, Rees, Orme, Brown, and Green.

———. |1814| 1951. *A philosophical essay on probabilities.* New York: Dover.

Larson, Edward J. 1985. *Trial and error.* New York: Oxford University Press.

Lester, Lane P., and Raymond G. Bohlin. 1984. *The natural limits to biological change.* Grand Rapids: Zondervan, Academie Books.

Ley, Willy. 1968. Introduction. In *Kant's cosmogony.* Trans. W. Haste. New York: Greenwood.

Lovejoy, Arthur O. |1936| 1960. *The great chain of being.* New York: Harper & Row.

Luther, Martin. 1967. *Table talk.* In *Luther's works.* Vol. 54. Ed. Theodore G. Tappert. Philadelphia: Fortress.

Lyell, Charles. |1830–33| 1887. *Principles of geology.* Vol. 1. New York: D. Appleton and Company.

McCosh, James, and George Dickie. 1856. *Typical forms and special ends in creation.* Edinburgh: Thomas Constable and Co.

McDonough, Thomas R. 1983, March/April. The search for extraterrestrial intelligence (SETI). *The Planetary Report.*

McGowan, Chris. 1984. *In the beginning.* Buffalo: Prometheus.

MacKay, Donald M. 1974. *The clock work image.* Downers Grove, Ill.: InterVarsity.

Maritain, Jacques. 1944. *The dream of Descartes.* Port Washington, N.Y.: Kennikat Press.

Matthews, L. Harrison. 1971. Introduction. In Charles Darwin's On *the origin of species.* London: Dent.

Mayr, Ernest. 1959. Introduction. In Charles Darwin's On *the origin of species.*

Mill, John Stuart. 1885. *Nature the utility of religion and theism.* London: Longmans, Green and Co.

Miller, Hugh. 1849. *Footprints of the creator.* Cited in Moore, James R. 1979. *The post-Darwinian controversies.* New York: Cambridge University Press. P. 205.

Montagu, Ashley, ed. 1984. *Science and creationism.* Oxford: Oxford University Press.

Moore, James R. 1979. *The post-Darwinian controversies.* New York: Cambridge University Press.

Morris, Henry M. 1966. *Studies in the Bible and science.* Grand Rapids: Baker.

———. 1983. *Science, Scripture, and the young earth.* El Cajon, Calif.: Institute for Creation Research.

_____, ed. 1974. *Scientific creationism*. San Diego: Creation-Life Publishers.

Newell, Norman D. 1982. *Creation and evolution*. New York: Columbia University Press.

Newton, Isaac. |1687| n.d. General Scholium. In *Mathematical principles of natural philosophy*. Great books of the western world series. Ed. Robert M. Hutchins. Vol. 34. Chicago: Encyclopaedia Brittannica.

Nowell-Smith, Patrick. 1955. Miracles. In *New essays in philosophical theology*. Ed. Antony Flew and Alasdair MacIntyre. New York: Macmillan.

Numbers, Ronald L. 1977. *Creation by natural law*. Seattle: University of Washington Press.

O'Neill, John J. 1980. *Prodigal genius*. Plymouth, Minn.: Washburn Press.

Orgel, Leslie. 1973. *The origins of life*. New York: Wiley.

Paley, William. |1802| 1963. *Natural theology*. Ed. Frederick Ferre. New York: Bobbs-Merrill.

Pierce, J. R. 1968, February. Information theory. *Bell Laboratories Record*.

Polanyi, Michael. 1967a, August 21. Life transcending physics and chemistry. *Chemical Engineering News*.

_____. 1967b. *The tacit dimension*. London: Routledge and Kegan Paul.

_____. 1968. Life's irreducible structure. *Science* 160: 1308.

Popper, Karl. 1976. *Unended quest*. LaSalle, Ill.: Open Court.

_____. 1980, August 21. Letter. *New Scientist*.

Rosenberg, Samuel I. Defendants' pre-trial brief: Senator Bill Keith against Louisiana Department of Education.

Rosenblum, Annette E. Letter to Charles Thaxton. 10–11–83.

Ruse, Michael. 1979. *The Darwinian revolution*. Chicago: University of Chicago Press.

_____. 1982. *Darwinism defended*. London: Addison-Wesley Publishing Company.

_____. 1984. A philosopher's day in court. In *Science and creationism*. Ed. Ashley Montagu. New York: Oxford University Press.

Russell, E. S. |1915| 1962. *The diversity of animals*. Cited in Moore, James R. 1979. *The post-Darwinian controversies*. New York: Oxford University Press.

Sagan, Carl. 1979. *Broca's brain*. New York: Random House.

_____. 1980. *Cosmos*. New York: Random House.

Sagan, Carl and I. S. Shklovskii. 1966. *Intelligent life in the universe*. San Francisco: Holden-Day.

Sandage, Allan. 1985. A scientist reflects on religious belief. *Truth*. Vol. 1. Dallas: Truth, Incorporated.

Science. 1982, February 29. Vol. 215.

Science and creationism, a view from the National Academy of Sciences. 1984. Washington, D.C.: National Academy Press.

Sheldrake, Rupert. 1981. *A new science of life*. Los Angeles: J. P. Tarcher.

Spinoza, Benedict. |1670; 1677| 1951. *A theologico-political treatise and A political treatise*. New York: Dover.

_____. |1677| 1953. *Ethics*. Ed. James Gutmann. New York: Hafner.

Stansfield, William. 1977. The science of evolution. New York: Macmillan. Cited in J. Gergman, Teaching about the creation/evolution controversy. *Fastback*, no. 134, 1979.

Sullivan, J. W. N. 1933. *The limitations of science*. New York: New American Library.

Teague, Olin E., chairman. 1977. *Possibility of intelligent life elsewhere in the universe*. Revised October 1977. Report prepared for the Committee on Science and Technology, U.S. House of Representatives. Washington, D.C.: U.S. Government Printing Office.

Thaxton, Charles. 1985. Christianity and the scientific enterprise. *Truth*, Vol. 1, pp. 61–64. Dallas: Truth, Incorporated.

Thaxton, Charles B., Walter L. Bradley, and Roger L. Olsen. 1984. *The mastery of life's origin*. New York: Philosophical Library.

Thomas Aquinas. 1945. *Basic writings of Saint Thomas Aquinas*. Ed. Anton C. Pegis. Vol. 1. New York: Random House.

Toulmin, Stephen, and June Goodfield. 1967. *The discovery of time*. Baltimore: Penguin.

Trefil, James S. 1983. Closing in on creation. *Smithsonian*.

Urey, Harold C. *The Christian Science Monitor*. January 4, 1962.

Wald, George. |1954| 1979. The origin of life. In *Life: Origin and evolution*. Introduction by T. E. Fulsom. San Francisco: Freeman.

Weizsacker, C. F. 1964. *The relevance of science*. New York: Harper and Row.

Whewell, William. |1857| 1967. *History of the inductive sciences*. Pt. 3. London: Frank Cass and Co.

White, Andrew Dickson. 1922. *A history of the warfare of science with theology in Christendom*. Vol. 1. New York: D. Appleton and Company.

Whitehead, Alfred North. 1925. *Science and the modern world*. New York: The Free Press.

_____. 1933. *Adventures of ideas*. New York: The Free Press.

Wilder-Smith, A. E. 1968. *Man's origin, man's destiny*. Minneapolis: Bethany Fellowship.

_____. 1980. *The natural sciences know nothing of evolution*. San Diego: Master Books.

Wilson, David B., ed. 1983. *Did the devil make Darwin do it?* Ames, Iowa: Iowa State University Press.

Wysong, R. L. 1976. *The creation-evolution controversy*. Midland, Mich.: Inquiry Press.

Yockey, Hubert P. 1981. Self organization origin of life scenarios and information theory. *Journal of Theoretical Biology*.

Index of Persons

Index of Subjects

Cosmogony, 62, 64, 69, 91, 112, 115
Cosmology, 57, 91, 112, 115, 118, 133
Creation, 19, 31, 35, 43, 45, 133, 151,
    152, 165, 167, 176; biochemical, 129;
    biological, 129; constitutionality of
    teaching about, 20–36, 175–77; old-
    earth view of, 154; "theory of," 83,
    147; young-earth view of, 153–54. *See
    also* Primary cause; Primary-cause
    theism; Total creation
Creation mandate, 40
Creation Research Society, 20
"Creation science," 165
Creator, 30, 33–35, 75, 84, 112 *See also*
    Design argument; Designer

Deduction, 39, 54
Deism, 91, 97, 122, 127
Design argument, 29, 140, 145, 146,
    156, 159–64
Designer, 30, 35, 72, 74. *See also* Creator
Deus ex machina, 28
Discontinuity, 121, 128
DNA, 142–45, 154–56, 161

Ecosystem, 154
Efficient cause, 29, 42, 123, 124, 143,
    147, 179. *See also* Primary cause;
    Secondary causes
Electrodynamics, 40
Empirical science, 17, 25, 36, 38, 43, 92,
    99, 134, 143, 179
Energetics, 40
Evolution: biochemical, 129; biological,
    23, 176; cosmic, 129; Greek view of,
    79. *See also* Natural selection
Evolutionary tree, 85, 151
Expanding universe, 117, 135
Experiment, 38, 41, 42, 48–49, 54, 92,
    112, 113

Falsification, 25, 125
Final cause, 42, 56, 58, 111, 123–26,
    131, 179
Forensic science, 25, 36, 106, 116
Formal cause, 42
Fossils, 86, 132, 150, 152–56. *See also*
    Geology; Paleontology
Four basic causes, 42

Genetic fallacy, 35
Genetics, 40
Geogony, 125
Geological column, 59. *See also* Fossils;
    Paleontology
Geology, 71, 73, 76–79, 89, 114, 120,
    125; glacial, 40
Gnosticism, 33
God-of-the-gaps, 17, 28, 65, 113–14
Gradualism, evolutionary, 152. *See also*
    Evolution; Macroevolution
Gravity, law of, 45, 50, 60, 65, 85
Greek view of science, 79–80, 111–12,
    179

Hinduism, 32, 36, 128, 165. *See also*
    Naturalistic evolution; Pantheism;
    Primary-cause naturalism
Historical geology, 14. *See also* Fossils;
    Paleontology
Hydrostatics, 39

Indeterminacy, principle of, 130
Induction, 42, 65
Infinite regress, 134
Information theory, 139, 142, 145, 162
Institute for Creation Research, 20
Instrumental cause, 50, 131
Intermediate forms, 152, 153
Investigator interference, 138
Irregular orbit of planets, 66
Islam, 36. *See also* Theism
Isotopic chemistry, 40

Judaism, 36. *See also* Theism

Law of gravitation. *See* Gravity, law of
Laws of nature, 96. *See also* Secondary
    causes
Laws, immutable, 95
Louisiana creation-evolution law, 20, 21,
    30, 175

Macroevolution, 15–18, 25, 26, 33, 108
Magnetic theory, 40
Markov process, 162
Materialistic perspective, 42, 93. *See also*
    Naturalism
Mathematical speculation, 44, 45, 64,
    65